Catharsis with Maa

OrangeBooks Publication

Smriti Nagar, Bhilai, Chhattisgarh - 490020

Website: **www.orangebooks.in**

© Copyright, 2023, Author

All rights reserved. No part of this book may be reproduced, stored in a retrieval system, or transmitted, in any form by any means, electronic, mechanical, magnetic, optical, chemical, manual, photocopying, recording or otherwise, without the prior written consent of its writer.

First Edition, 2023
ISBN: 978-93-5621-691-4

Catharsis with Maa

Through language and society, space and time, life and death

Agniva Pal

OrangeBooks Publication
www.orangebooks.in

Dedicated to the dead, dedicated to the living.
Dedicated to flora and fauna.
Dedicated to the vibrant and dull.
Dedicated to the past and the future.
Dedicated to you.
'Maa'
Dadu[1]
Bhaiyo Dadu[2]
Dimma[3]
Boromama[4]

---

[1] Dadu – The author's father's father. The author's paternal grandfather.

[2] Bhaiyo Dadu – The author's mother's father. The author's maternal grandfather.

[3] Dimma – Shortened form of Didima. The author's mother's mother. The author's maternal grandmother.

[4] Boromama – The author's mother's eldest brother. The author's maternal uncle.

Acknowledgements

I regret every moment. I regret every moment I could have spent with Maa; the mother, who taught me to drink, to eat, to laugh, to cry but not a lot, to feel, to see, to see with clarity, to hear, to hear with reason and parity, to reason, to breathe, to touch, to feel, to sympathise and empathize and to be what I am. An acknowledgement is the one portion in a book, people skip because it's not part of a story but it is here that the most gracious thank yous are given to the people who mean a lot to every little or big hand who lent out some sort of help, sympathy or empathy.

Let me start with Maa. I seem to be not be able to do anything without her and yet now I have to do everything without her. I thank her for making me a fine young man. I thank her for giving me a mind that reasons, fights, questions, respects and a mind that can bear, opinionate and silence! I thank Maa for making me what I am. I would be nothing without her. The thin yet strong spider wool steel thread that connects my stories together is Maa. She is the cohesion and adhesion of my story. I thank her.

Baba, you've been nothing short of being too supportive and not too supportive for my own good. You've been there whenever I've needed you. True that you've at times tried to fill in the shoes of Maa by trying to do things you never did, but that is not needed. You've done enough and will do enough. This, I know. There will never be a time when I'll not need you and there will never be a time when I'll despise you. You've also inspired me to be the teacher I am now and to go ahead with life, after Maa, with my head held high, without tears in my eyes. Thank you Baba.

Tulika, you have been my constant support. I remember the way I broke down 22 March onwards (not that I don't now) and the way you literally made me stand up once again, pick up my pieces and continue with my life. You reminded me that life has to go on and that life must not stop. You are my corner stone.

Tua, you've been the little puzzle of happiness I always loved as my own. You've been there with Maa when I was here and Baba was at his workplace. You've been the person who spent time with Maa, just like I did when I was young. It was very difficult to replace me. Turns out, Maa had reserves of love available for both of us; reserves we both miss now. Thank you for being the amazing little sister.

Kaku, Kakima and Amma have always been the cornerstone of our family. I shall go back home now, to my family, when I do, to be with them. Maa's leaving us, has given me one less reason to go back home and settle there. Thank you for inspiring me to be better than what I am now. Thank you for being there.

I've been teaching for the last 3 years and a few months, give or take. I've come across some amazing souls I've loved teaching and learnt with them, as well as taught them. Thank you Aastha for taking the time to read my book. Thank you for telling me that you loved my story and thank you for pointing out the mistakes. Thank you sincerely. Thank you Manisha for inspiring me. You told me that a little soul like me can also be inspired to publish his own book. And here I'm still writing. Thank you Ranjani and Sneha for reading excerpts from my book and explaining to me which genre it should ideally fall into. Thank you, all my students, for being there for me, for listening to me, for helping me be the teacher I'm now.

I would like to thank everyone who has a role in making this book a success! I know it will be, given the amazing hands of people behind it and supporting it. Thank you everyone.

Love,
Agniva

Table of Contents

Synopsis 1
One that was originally planned for the back of
the book but was over-written

**Explanations/ Annotations of Some
Terms Used in the Book** 4
Grab a cup of coffee and pen and paper;
these are important names in the author's life

Dear Baba 9
A letter from the author to his father;
an epistle about life; a preface

Let there be Sense 12
And there was knowledge; a preface from the author

Time Stood Still 18
A Preface from the author's father Achintya Kumar Pal;
Baba writes

Time: the Quintessential Ingredient for Life 29
Since my writing talks about impermanence of time; a
preface by Adrija Pal, the author's sister

A Preface From the Author's Fiance 36

Introducing Dr. Rita Barai 38
Act 1 scene 1: enter mom, my Maa,
my world, my universe! 38

Day Zero – Predestination 41
The day my life changed forever

Day Zero – Memories of a Past Life 50
The other side of the day

Day 1 59
The illusion of control

Day 2 71
The nights are when it's the most difficult

Day 3 77
The system failed her

Beautiful Lies 83
11 years back, through Maa's eyes; her story

Day 4 89
So what is life anyway? What is faith? What is belief?

Day 5 96
The day hundreds cried at her memorial

Day 6 100
It's a new world out there

Coping Mechanisms 103
Everybody has their own

Day 7 107
One week since incident

Day 8 112
She didn't know

Day 9 114
Trying to smile while my world just died!

Day 10 119
I remember how she spoke, how she laughed

Day 11 125
Much loved characters are seldom real

Day 12 129
I can't pretend to be fine anymore

Day 13 134
There's a smell of false spontaneity to everything

Day 14 143
Two weeks later

Day 15 150
My eyes opened and there I was, still on my bed

Day 17 155
I can feel the paradigmatic exigencies
changing around me

Of Indelible Pains and Endless Cacophony 159
The last few minutes

Maa's Mornings 163
A typical morning in Maa's day

That One Time I Died 167
And the memories I never had from the eyes of Maa; with a hint of Tagore

Day 21 175
Epistles which will never reach you

Everything is relative 183
And we are just pawns in the
brief period of time we live in

Memories 186
I have this intense passionate desire
to go back to being young again

Why I Hate Birthdays and Spring! 191
And why they make me sad

A Series of Unfortunate Events 193
That led to what should not have happened

Fur One More Time! 196
Once upon a time in a family from a faraway galaxy on a
string vibrating to a different frequency

~~His~~ Her- Story 202
Breaking stereotypes, gender roles and
unneeded traditions, one signified at a time

The Paradise 205
That became a civilized mess

She Was Crying Absolutely Helplessly 208
When I walked in

The Curious Case of the Bucketing Meniscus 211
When the meniscus in my knee decided to take a vacation

Childhood 213
From the earliest on memories I have

Day 30 216
Exactly one month after her demise

Too Little Too Soon 220
Little did I know that I would never see her again,
in person

The Microcosm of the Belief System 224
Everything is theoretically impossible until it is done

The Me That Never Was 229
Sometimes I wish I could talk to her

That One Time 233
A time which will never be or was

Of Life and Death 237
Society thinks

The Eulogy No One Wants 241
Disintegrated into a million parts

Once Upon a Time 244
The light at the end of the tunnel

And This is to Go Beyond 251
I don't mean for you to read or watch more
but you may find these interesting

Synopsis

One that was originally planned for the back of the book but was over-written...

Written from an autobiographical perspective, the book deep dives into questions about life, origins of life, death and what death is, although from a biological and physics point of view; not philosophical. This book moves from page to page describing how the author has spent his days after he lost his mother on the 22 of March, 2022. Perspectives, outlooks and horizons changed for the author the moment his mother died.

This is a journey of learning, re-learning and un-learning life decisions, habits through an uncanny pedagogical point of view. Being an assistant professor himself, he best finds the story being narrated from a pedagogical point of view, with educational anecdotes, digressions and lessons on life from physics, chemistry, biology and linguistics. Every chapter delves into 'days in the life' of the author and gives immaculate details of how they have been spent. The author believes in making the readers feel the emotions he went through, making them kinaesthetic to the activities, making the readers see the things he saw and then in turn transporting them to a world he lived in. This book starts on the day he lost his mother and ends on an open ended note, letting the readers delve deep into questions about 'death', 'after-life' from a pedagogical point of view.

Education in today's age is at best compartmentalised, theatrically driven and lacks pedagogical ingenuity. The reason we come across the names of famous philosophers, as we peruse through subjects we have studied and loved (or probably pursued for the degree) is because once upon a time there was no segregation amongst subjects. True that division of labour had already come into existence, as human beings started living in groups of more than 150 odd numbers but even at that time, a hunter could wonder about the apparent movement of the sun and the moon, navigate their way by looking at the stars; a good cook might also wonder about how people died and so on. In the modern world adorned by social media stimulus beyond actual humanistic probabilities, we have grown into aggressively social yet unsocial islands governed by ruling binary oppositions. A lawyer does not look up at the sky anymore to ask questions about the stars. An engineer rarely watches a film and wonders how the relationship depicted in the film could give them catharsis. A doctor rarely has time to breathe, let alone wonder about things. A teacher limits themselves to their own subjects and other subjects are seldom even spoken about and as a species, we have been systematically cordoning ourselves from everything. The author's world was different. Throughout his childhood, he has been made to question, ponder and systematically trained to untrain himself in the ways of the world. Though he is no rebel, he still questions, studies and occasionally takes up reading about multiple disciplines and uses them to teach.

This book, though a memoir to the death of the author's mother is also be a window into the mind of the author. Thoughts, desires, aspirations, inspirations and a lifetime of memories; everything is in this book. It is the author's way of keeping his 'Maa' alive through his own words! He will never get back his 'Maa' but she will be immortalised through his writing.

The book goes about in a linear approach, starting on the day the author lost his mother, moving ahead as days pass after his mother's death. As days fly by, the author drowns himself in memories of times before, somewhat akin to the stream of consciousness technique at times.

Explanations/ Annotations of Some Terms Used in the Book

Grab a cup of coffee and pen and paper; these are important names in the author's life

- Maa – Means mother in most languages. In this book, it refers to me calling my mother in my narratives; the mother that doesn't exist anymore for me; the one that has left me and has prompted me to emote through this book.

- Baba – The patriarch in a typical Indian family; the dad; in this book my father.

- Rubbai – My father or Baba used to call my mother or Maa, Rubbai. Originally Maa's grandfather used to call her this. Baba took up this name because Maa loved it.

- Tata/ Tatai – A character from Rabindranath Tagore's story 'Rajorshi' where 'Tata' and 'Hashi' are siblings. I have been referred to as 'Tata' by Maa and Baba due to their immense love for Tagore. Variations include Tata and Tatai.

- Amma – The mother of my father; my grandmom.

- Dadu – The father of Baba; the husband of Amma; the father-in-law of my Maa.

- Kaku – Brothers (any of them, including the biological one) of my father; uncle in simpler terms. There are plenty of uncles in the extended family including the biological one.

- Kakima – Wives of any of the Kaku-s; mostly refers to the wife of my Kaku's (biological brother of my father) wife.

- Tulika – The author's fiancé, my fiancé.

- Tua – My little sister. The daughter of my father's biological brother; Kaku.

- Dada – Tua calls me Dada. Dada is a word for elder brother in the language 'Bangla'.

- Babui – My father, my Baba calls me Babui.

- Tingling, Biskittie, Le Brew, Bagha, Blackie – dogs we have loved over the years.

- Alice – A German shepherd I have grown up with; equally loved by Maa.

- Acche din – A day Indians still wait for just like Vladimir and Estragon still wait for Godot. They are still waiting; aren't they?

- Holud Pakhi – A famous song by Cactus, a Bangla band, available on YouTube. I used to sing it when I was a kid. Maa loved it. Now it is a memory of how we used to spend times.

- Mamabari – The original home Maa. In a typical Indian wedding, women leave their homes and belongings as if they never mattered, to leave for her newlywed husband's place leaving everything; in some cases, even their original names. Maa's original home was Mamabari.

- Masimoni – The elder sister of Maa.

- Chotomama – The immediate elder brother of Maa.

- Boromama – The eldest most brother of Maa.

- Chinsurah – A city in which I grew up; located in West Bengal, India. Unlike allegorical towns, this city is absolutely real, with real people, real voices and real problems. It was settled in by the Dutch while the rest of India was under the British. It ultimately fell into British hands though and it has tales to tell. Visit it someday!

- Gurgaon/ Gurugram – A major city adjacent to Delhi; a city with sprinkles of the ancient Aravalli range. It is a city in which the author currently resides. It's a city from the inside but the native people anthropologically haven't been able to leave their hunter gatherer/ farmer tenant mentality behind. It's a village in the guise of a town. Must visit. Recommended!

- Chandannagore – A town next to Chinsurah. It was a French settlement and it never fell in British hands. It gained freedom from the French in the 1960s. This was where the author's Maa last worked at, before her demise.

- Khalisani – A small part of Chandannagore, still untouched mostly by promoters hungry for land money.

- Scooty – A two wheeled moped with an Internal combustion engine Maa used.

- Bansberia – A town near Chinsurah. This was Maa worked for 11 years.

- Siliguri – A large town in the Northern part of West Bengal, near the Himalayas. Maa lived her last days here, in a hospital, half-dead in a swoon.

- Mummum – I used to call Maa, Mummum when I was young. Tua started to call Maa as Mummum later on. Baba also calls Tua Mummum.

- Ranaghat – A town in Nadia, West Bengal. A town in Maa breathed her last. This town will always haunt me as the town where Maa died.

- Sandakfu – Basecamp town for Kanchenjunga treks and a beautiful location to watch the mountain from. This was where the author's Maa went to visit on her last journey in life.

- Sattal – A small town in Uttarakhand state in India, this is also a heaven for birdwatcher's. The author's Maa loved this place.

- Bheemtal – Another small town in Uttarakhand state in India, named after the lake it houses.

- Papa – Tulika calls her father Papa.

Dear Baba

A letter from the author to his father;
an epistle about life; a preface

Dear Baba,

The world did not end when the person you and I loved the most died. Instead, the world became a bed of memories, instances, pictures, songs, trips and videos of her. I understand it's very difficult for you right now, having been with her for almost forty two years, through thick and thin through war and peace through recession and inflation, through grief and happiness. You've lived with her being her support and while I took away your thunder after I was born, I know for a fact that she loved you dearly. Dear Baba, the world will go on like it was yesterday, like it was the day some fateful amino acids mixed up to form the first life in some soup in a part of Africa and the world will go on like it did after thousands died in the second covid wave in India (well, lakhs). Dear Baba, we will keep on subconsciously imagining her existence in her life for a long time now and probably forever. In the beginning there will only be tears, but just like all cognizant beings, after some time we will only turn back to the happy parts. We will definitely miss your Rubbai and my Maaaaa every hour of the day and definitely when we are sick and need a doctor but in the end, we will be left with beautiful memories which will give us haunting yet relieving flashbacks. Dear Baba, you are not alone. It is true that you have lost your soulmate and I, my Maa but we are together in this. We lost our best friend and we are down from a trio to a duo. I know we are not together right now, while I am writing this but I promise you, I am finding a way to get back home, soon! Stop blaming yourself, till then. Please!

I have always wanted to write a book. I have never understood how people write novels and how they manage to outsource so many words and stories from their puny little brains. Now, when Maa is gone, the pain of losing her has inevitably pushed me into emptying my thoughts through writing. I used to wet my pants when I was a child and Maa used to help me change. Now Maa is gone and I am back to wetting my bed; although with tears this time around. I've explored an abundance of things I've been questioning myself about. I have explored and touched upon concepts of self and self-awareness, concepts of life and death but in no specific order; and through examples from recent incidences.

I was not ready to lose Maa. No one was. I've never been able to share my true emotions with you, in spite of being so close to you. As they say, I'm a closed person. I shut out people. I have always been apathetic to questions about me and my feelings from both of you but I am happy Maa knew how much I loved her.

Baba, someday we will both die. We will both have people left in this world to cry for us and we will have our legacies being lived by our progenies (I being yours and Maa's). Life, since the moment those amino acids formed the first life, has been trying to stay alive through various means. For higher primates like us, it is passing on the DNA to the next generation through nature and then giving them upbringing they need to become like us, through nurture!

This is me trying to emote, trying to break free of a flux of emotionless, cold tragedy. We share a lot Baba but in the end of this, maybe lies our little, personal, beautiful closure.

Love,
Babui

Let there be Sense

And there was knowledge;
a preface from the author

In the beginning there was nothing. It all started with a singularity and then there as the big bang, without a Cherenkov radiation[5] because it was space that expanded in the first place. Everything as we know came into existence.

I would love to believe I belong to a higher plane of existence, one in which I am not a prisoner of the fourth dimension we allude to as, 'time'.

I would love to believe that I belong to a plane of existence where I can freely move into time, just like I can move out of my drawing room into my bedroom.

---

[5] Cherenkov radiation – electromagnetic radiation emitted due to particles moving faster than light in situations where the speed of light is retarded due to travel inside a medium unlike vacuum. It is a sonic boom for light.

Time is a notion created by man to provide meaning to the chain of causalities happening around them. Time and space are inseparable. Time and space are one!

What we think is the end, might just be the beginning. No, it is not a philosophical outlook which enables me to say this but rather empirical reasoning[6]. Everything we see around us, is in plenty. Elements, compounds, life and species, Rocky planets[7], asteroids, gas giant planets[8], comets from the Oort cloud[9], stars of various sizes and ages and the variety and multiplicity in them, the galaxies, the nebulae; everything has instances of themselves being replicated and are in existence.

With the kind of existential proof we have for various things, what makes us think that there is only one Universe and that there is no second version of me, probably not a lifeform based on carbon, in another universe, now happily spending time with his family,

---

[6] Empirical reasoning – A certain way of thought process (mostly used in research) which involves and includes decisions in life or in research based on inputs from the five senses.

[7] Mercury, Venus, Earth and Mars are the rocky planets in the solar system

[8] Jupiter, Saturn, Uranus, Neptune are the gas giants in the solar system.

[9] Oort Cloud – a belt of icy comets and asteroids beyond the orbit of Pluto (pluto is no longer a planet. Jupiter has moons much larger than Pluto. Alas! Pluto!)

where his Maa is still alive! What makes us think that the question I've put forward is more philosophical than realistic and astronomical?

Our limitations are binding and whatever we see, feel, touch, smell, hear are empirical reason enough for us to work on scientific developments. What most of us fail to consider is that most of the daily truths of facts we believe in are contained to the regions on earth we are confined to in space and in time.

We are delimited by our little lives, to live and die, like cogs in a machine, not think beyond our specific understanding and observable universe (here I refer to not the astronomical observable universe but to the parole of confinement we limit ourselves to everyday).

We are delimited by our thoughts stemming out of the parole[10] we use every day and we die with our little brains, not knowing most (mostly all) of what is beyond our little sphere of observable universe. We call that life.

---

[10] Parole – parts of language we use in our own lives (language, stored knowledge – both in memory and books, utterances, traditions, cultural cues and so on)

What if we could be beings with access to the Tesseract[11], not the Marvel cinematic universe[12] kind but the geometric concept of the Tesseract, which is a cube with each of its faces being replaced with cubes, a figure possible only we move to a place of existence with four dimensions. We would then have access to time as we have access to the x, y and z dimensions, that is, access to sidewise motion, back and forth motion and up and down height wise motion. The fourth dimension would then suddenly open to us. Our stream of consciousness[13], even if it has always allowed us to sneakily move in and out of time, as if it were another room, is just a figment of our imagination. It is but a sad supernova that we are indeed limited to the three dimensions of travel while our mind is capable of such greater lengths. Time would not flow, anymore in one dimension. There would be no present,

---

[11] Tessaract – a geometric figure possible when you replace all the faces of a cube with cubes. A tesseract is to a cube, what a cube is to a square. Imagine replacing all the square faces on a cube, with cubes themselves. It is only possible if we move beyond the 3 dimensions we live in, into a higher plane of existence.

[12] A nod to the blue cube, a specific stone in the Marvel Cinematic Universe holding amazing powers.

[13] Stream of consciousness – a technique generally referring to the way our human minds think, jumping from thought to though in a non-linear pattern; incoherent to anyone but the user.

past or future times. There would be no concept of flowing time.

A higher dimension would then enable us to navigate through time and be able to cross the inundate barrier, like we can't do with time, now. We would be able to visit the big bang[14] or the big crunch[15].

We would be able to visit the primal soup of organic molecules which gave birth to the first life on planet earth (given the conditions through which life has sustained itself, including five mass extinction events and the Holocene anthropogenic extinction event[16] going on now, I would indeed believe that life beyond earth exists; we are just too young as a species to have explored so far). We would be able to see the largest crustaceans and the smallest virus being born as a probable mutation of a bacteria which wanted to evolve into a lazier form.

---

[14] The probable rational and astrophysical, astronomical start of the universe

[15] The probable rational and astrophysical, astronomical end of the universe

[16] Holocene anthropogenic extinction event – induced mass extinction due to the intervention of human beings in everything. The destruction of forests, the over pollutive nature, the overuse of carbon and so on so forth are leading to a mass extinction seen in the K-Pg event 66 million years ago.

We would be able to visit the time when post-humanism would be at its peak and we would be half the humans we are. I would be able to visit Maa, just like I did every day. Maa would exist, not on this planet of existence but on another where she is always taking birth and always dying.

The fourth dimension would be accessible and time, as we know now, would stop existing.

"Evolution may be progressive or retrogressive. The necessity is living a decent life, which we can term survival. Survival does not always mean to be fittest by struggle.
You can survive well just by becoming humble and by shredding all decorations, we feel aren't necessary!"

- Baba (Achintya Kumar Pal)

Time Stood Still

A Preface from the author's father Achintya Kumar Pal; Baba writes

তদেজেতি তন্নৈজেতি তদ্দূরে তদ্বন্তিকে।

তদন্তরস্য সর্বস্য তদু সর্বস্যাস্য বাহ্যত॥

"She moves, she doesn't move. She is far away and yet near.
She is inside of everyone and she is outside everyone."

In the moments I knew that I lost my Rubbai, a realisation dawned upon me. It was in fact an unmeasurable span of time, a span of time in which I had lost all perception, all emotions, all expressions and all language.

It was indeed a moment in space and time, everything stood still.

Her dull and tired, sad and moist eyes were fixed on me and she looked at me, as if to express something. She was struggling to breathe in spite of oxygen being pumped by the BiPAP[17] machine and the paramedics in the ambulance rushed her to the emergency in the nearest hospital on the same stretcher; the one in the ambulance; on which she lied down for the last twelve hours.

I faintly remember someone calling me to complete the formalities for her admission to the intensive care unit at the medical facility and I recall the sounds of instruments, fragmented instructions of attending doctors and the distant existence of the woman I love, lying on bed in an emergency ward, away from home, away from the dirge and murmurs of a city, struggling for her life. At that moment in time, I had known her for forty two long years; a time in which she had wrapped me in her care and love.

I, like any of my homo sapiens cousins have made innumerable mistakes and any one of those silly or major reasons, would have been enough to end her care, love and understanding for me. She silently imbibed my behaviour, brushed through all my negligence and selfishness and smiled at me even at a juncture of intense lack of care for her on my part.

We were close but we also went through many phases. Sometimes we were inseparable and sometimes we fought. I loved her though. She had this in her WhatsApp status, a line by Tagore, "দিনে দিনে কঠিন হলো কখন বুকের তল" (My heart has slowly turned into stone as time has

---

[17] BiPAP - breathing support administered through a face mask, nasal mask, or a helmet without putting tubes inside.

passed). It was one of those times when I was facing an odd predicament and time threw me on the sandy deserted banks of life. It was poetic, her WhatsApp status. I wish we made up soon after though. I wish we did not fight the number of times we did, throughout our lives. I wish all the times we fought, we spent time together, pondering about the cosmos, thinking about our son and his future and wandering the planet we live on. I didn't realise all the times we fought would haunt me, after! I considered asking her to change her tag line many a times, but helplessly withdrew into my broken shell. She was a matriarch and historically speaking she changed her mind only when she had enough reason to do so. She had reasons to! As we went through the vicissitudes of life together, time and again, time and space around us again offered us unfettered chances for us to grab windows into feeling serenity of closeness in us again. Our son, Tatai, has grown up to be a decent man and he and his cousin, my brother's daughter (rather our daughter too; relations aren't determined by nature, but by nurture) Tua, bent our reality to make us run collide from being parallel lines which never meet, away from our once drifted away existence.

Tuli, then walked into my son's life. This young woman shared so many signature characteristics of Rubbai, that it was uncanny. Oedipus complex! Maybe! She absolutely rivetted the gap between us, as we started planning the wedding of Tatai and Tuli. Rubbai eventually turned back into a little girl I met in a class of meritorious students, aspiring for bright futures ahead. This was when the Naxalite movement was just over and the leftist movement was trying to bring about an Utopian social equality beating the stagnant rightist scenario of socio-political West Bengal.

When we first met, we studied biological science together but she extended her help to me, for other science subjects as well. I started to accompany her to her recitation competitions and she was so good, she would always claim one of the first three positions.

We were then, what you may call, dependent friends. We had our differences as well (probably why we had fights but as they say, opposites attract). She was the voice, while I was the background artist.

I loved supporting her while she looked forward to my support. I preferred to stay behind her, unlike patriarchs, but she, on the other hand, would keep me by her side in decisions, in emotions and in life.

When it gets to being pawned, here is a story. We were the second batch of 10+2[18] system of education; innocent guinea pigs subjected to experiments by the government. We had to spend a lot of time in libraries as there was no text books.

---

[18] A prevalent education system in India which follows one board exam in the 10th standard followed by another in the 12th standard, following which one makes it to college education starting with Bachelor's degree.

Authors were still writing them and the education system, although strong, was still at infancy. The syllabus, a piece of paper with all that we had to study, always changing and always being edited; did not help much and stayed mostly with our teachers. We, henceforth had to explore a lot of books for graduate studies.

We spent a lot of time together and she eventually became a member in our then non-digital family. The world was very different then. We had letters to write and books to read and discuss, and we did it with pleasure. We exchanged thoughts that germinated through layers of pages, without the need for emoticons. We had vast worlds of imagination which helped us observe and yet not fixate on 30 seconds of immediate entertainment available on most social media platforms today. We, also, knew nothing about the ecstasy of touching each other though. We grew up in an age of binary oppositions without too many gradients[19].

It took more than a year for me to come to the understanding that I needed her for my survival, and for me to inform her was as improbable as climbing the monstrous K2 mountain, without even a little bit knowledge of rock climbing. Her acceptance came like

---

[19] A subtle reference to post structuralism and deconstruction. Language and perception have been seen to denote binaries in it and around us. Human beings have been perceiving the world through binaries; e.g. Good and bad, cold and hot and so on.

Harry's letter[20], delivered by the owl. She accepted to share her genes with mine, on the eve of my birthday and gifted me a card she had painted a wish on, " আমি তব মালঞ্চের হব মালাকর" (I will be the gardener to your flowers; beautiful lines from Tagore). I have lost the card now but the memories remain, engraved in my mind. She became the world I live in and praise. That was the enchanted sentence that she had promised once and forever. I have had digressions from the promise I had made to her, but she was the immovable object; resolute and bold; she never broke hers!

We were different. In an age where ritualistic praying was on the rise, we questioned the existence and efficacy of higher powers. Being the empiricists we are, the rituals in our marriage lasted ten minutes. Some people were shocked. Some were offended. Some were happy they did not have to wait very long. But, we were just happy that we got married.

We belong to the middle class. We did not have a lot of money to spend. Flashbacks of her bridal make up, still emblazons me today with fond memories. I was mesmerised when I first saw her that day. I was told that she would dress up elegantly on our wedding day but that day things looked pretty different. She told me earlier that she would dress elegantly, on our wedding day, as she used to do when we first met, but she had better plans. She

---

[20] A reference to Harry Potter by J.K Rowling

did so much more. Had it not been for Shyamal[21], I would not have the exquisite pictures of Rubbai, I have now, from the day of our wedding. There were several prewedding photographs of ours, shot in a time period of over thirteen years[22] of our acquaintance before the wedding. I have always loved photography and she was my first portrait model. She had loved for me to have clicked her photographs. Memory brings me to the last photograph I clicked of her on the trip to Sandakfu. She looked so happy! When Tatai walked into our world, the focus was shifted to him (It was temporary though. When he left home for his higher studies, we were left alone again. It is a cruel world.) accompanying his loving mother. He has in his possession, all the albums of his childhood and he still looks at them at times.

When it gets to earning, I have always tried to do it honestly. When we got married, she was in government service as a medical officer and carried the financial burden of our entire family. My father was earning pension, but that was not enough to run our joint family. She kept supporting the family, while offering medical help to thousands as a doctor.

---

[21] Shyamal Uncle – A very close friend of the author's Baba at that time. Probably the author's father had his first taste in photography as a result of this association.

[22] The author's parents courted each other for 13 years before they got married.

Catharsis with Maa

Time rushed by and soon I had the opportunity to share the ecstasy of receiving my appointment letter from 'West Bengal Education Service' with Ru and Baba. It was the March of 1999. My father was so glad that I had gotten over the gloomy days in my life, finally landing a government job; a stable job. Things were moving ahead well and there were no blemishes!

Barely weeks had passed by from the time I had received my letter from the government service and Baba lost his life to a massive global cerebral stroke. We had minutes at best. He never allowed us time to do anything. Ru and I rushed him to the hospital but he had already succumbed to the massive stroke. Baba loved me, depended on me, like I depend on my son now. June 1999, he suddenly stopped existing. Every experience, every touch, every smell, every vision, every audible remembrance was gone. What remained, were memories and tears. It was just months before

I would have joined the service and Baba did not give me the opportunity to share my glee with him, on joining the job. It was a major setback but Ru helped me overcome it. She helped balance the social rituals and covered my faithlessness in it with her smiles. Now that I think of it, it is very déjà vu-ish how Rubbai has left us, right before Tatai gets married with Tuli. It is unfortunate that my son, who loved Ru[23] so much, will never be able to share his

---

[23] Ru – shortened form of Rubbai, a name the author's Baba called the author's Maa.

happiness with his mother. I will be there but I do not that would be enough.

Baba thought he was lucky that he could see Tatai, his grandchild. His ancestors for the last few generations could not see their grandchildren, due to their untimely deaths. Rubbai was treated as a torch bearer; one who had given birth to a son. She was the flag bearer who was guiding our family, albeit without phenotypical dominance[24]. My family gradually got acquainted to a perfect balance between ritualistic and scientific practices. And although I finally got the freedom to plunge myself into my job as Ru kept Tatai company, teaching the subject I have loved all along, we slowly drifted away from each other. Time has this phenotypical yet tactical destructive nature, tacit to it.

The new millennium was here and I found that my son had decided to pursue humanities in his 10+2 in spite of having enough marks to take up sciences. We did not stop him. Rubbai provided him ample space and guidance for him to avail the freedom of achieving academic success. Oh, how I still remember this grown up man taking birth from Rubbai, on a rainy day.

We had planned to live out our retirement life visiting different corners of our country while helping our son raise his next gen, but alas, no more! She had carefully

---

[24] Phenotypical dominance – dominance through any observable characteristics of the body or mind.

crafted a niche holding our family together. She had grand plans to enjoy Tatai and Tuli's wedding with friends, family members and colleagues, in December 2022. And soon after this, she had plans for us, senior citizens. She had planned to visit Norway only to enjoy the nature's mysticism and the eternal ceremony of colours - aurora borealis. It's in March when this natural event can be seen the best. Did she really plan for me to enjoy this alone? How can I do this alone? I do not have enough balloons to lift my house 'Up'[25]!

I don't believe that she was happy to have left me abruptly at dawn on 22 March 2022. That day she did not adore her flowering plants, orchids, succulents and the birds in her terrace garden. No one was ready for this. My son, daughter and my daughter in law suffered the death of their best friend. But Rubbai left back so many other people in pain. Her batchmates, colleagues, patients or even common human beings helped by her and others who just saw her once, remember her with her smile, as a benevolent Goddess. I don't believe in resurrection, as I know this is a finite world with time which flows in one direction and I empirically discern that the elements that make our existence do not reassemble magically, following an 'already-in-place' plan to play its role in mortal world again, as a different character. Any life happens once. There are no recurrences. But I also believe there is a parallel world, where another Rubbai and her companion, me (or maybe not me) are still enjoying their

---

[25] A nod to the movie Up, by Pixar, Disney.

lives and preparing for the marriage of their son; the dream occasion for which she kept on shopping sarees after sarees and jewellery after jewellery for. This would be the only possible time and occasion when this probable character would have had accepted money from the other me, for the first time in their conjugal life. Does this other she still smile? What will she wear on the wedding? Does she still recite Tagore in all her emotions? Does her Whatsapp tag line still read the same? Does she breathe?

Time: the Quintessential Ingredient for Life

Since my writing talks about impermanence of time; a preface by Adrija Pal, the author's sister

We as human beings have stumbled upon various questions regarding countless topics that arouse our innate curiosity and consciousness as the 'superior beings'. It is safe to say that although we have not been successful in clarifying all our doubts, we as the only human civilization, have come quite far. A lot of progress has been made. Be it scientifically, evolutionarily, technologically or the as the human society as a whole, we have transformed ourselves from the once 'Archaic Humans' to the so called modern beings of the 21st century. However there are questions that still keeps us rethinking about our consciousness at times. No scientific reasoning or logic seems enough to satisfy our inquisitiveness. Life and death are such topics that create an unknown fear among us, resulting from our incapacity to form a concrete reason of our existence. Over centuries, scientists, physicists, biologists and even philosophers have given their own versions of what life and death can be, but the emptiness still continues to remain. What is life? Why are we even alive? What is the purpose of life? Does it hold any meaning? If it doesn't, what is the point of even living? What does death feel like? What happens after death? Is there an afterlife? These questions often make us fall into deep rabbit hole named 'existential crisis'. Being unable to find the ultimate truth, we mostly start 'believing'; believing in ideas of the 'supreme deity', the one and only force that commands our universe and other such ideas arising from different religious and spiritual backgrounds, hoping to find solace and comfort in this bleak and desolate arena of our curiosity. We become so connected and madly devoted to our beliefs and ideologies that all other possible explanations seem conflicting and contradictory. There exists a humongous disparity in thoughts and beliefs among people regarding the universe, it's laws and the presence of an omnipotent celestial being. It is due to this clash of ideas and fragile egos that humankind is hindered from exploring beyond their existing knowledge. They fail to find the ultimate truth because of their everlasting tussle between faith and belief. However while doing so we tend to forget that time is transient. It is time that binds life and death, good and bad, and war and peace. We believe that we can see all the wonders of the world, conquer the toughest terrains, eat exotic delicacies, meet interesting people, fall in love (and not consequently but probably fall out of it), grow old together with our surroundings and finally bid adieu to this mortal world leaving behind footprints for our next generations. But it is time that destroys this utopic idea of life by bringing unexpected hurdles along our path. It is the only thing capable of giving us excessive joy through the creation of life and also unexplainable sadness through the end of it.

The greatest mystery of life perhaps remains in the fact that our birth is unpredictable and sometimes a great privilege. Even though we can control a lot of things in our lives as we progress and establish ourselves, we really cannot prophesise our birth. Be it a millionaire's son or a homeless man's daughter, none in this case have a choice. The unborn cannot choose it's parents, family or its surroundings. A foetus cannot anticipate what the future has in store for it, what kind of love and affection will it receive and how the journey of life will be. When I was a foetus inside my mother, I never thought that I would be blessed with a family that loves and cherishes me the most and bonds stronger than the atoms in an element. It never occurred to me that I would be privileged enough to meet a human as special as 'Mummum' and she would be the first person to bring me to this beautiful world from my mother's womb. It is from this day we had a connection - an unexplainable bond that one can only dream of, an aunt who is nothing less than a mother figure, rather my second mother. We often say that a parent's love knows no bounds and hence has no alternative to it. While this is absolutely true, I also believe that love is not unidirectional or uniform. In our short-lived journey, we meet thousands of people who only have the role of being passers-by, thereby neither influencing us nor having a deep impact in our lives. But there are a chosen few, whose love feels like the warmest hug in a freezing day, whose company is irreplaceable and impact unfathomable. Their love is pure and unconditional.

Mummum was such a person in my life, constantly looking out for me, loving, caring and acting as a shade in which I can rest and a support I can rely on. My life would be entirely different, probably like a building with a weak foundation, had she not been there since the beginning.

Recalling our memories together is both a delight and a sorrow. Delightful since it makes me cherish all the moments we have spent together gossiping and bantering about the daily humdrums of life, laughing endlessly at the most trivial things, those meaningless conversations and countless travel journeys of which I have been a part of till the last day. However, all those moments can never be rewinded. Never will I get the chance to accompany her in the sudden trips to the greeneries, the frequent visits to the evergreen jungles blooming with flowers and filled with exotic birds and animals; the seminars, the wedding receptions and every other place where she has taken me to. Moreover so, she would also not miss any opportunity to reprimand me for my silly and intentional mistakes, recklessness and absent-mindedness. The so called 'bad habits' in the name of hygiene, manners and an overall casual approach towards life without any concrete goal, was what angered her about me. But it is now that I understand that every lashing was intended for my own good, because she cared enough to look through my faults and correct them. It felt good to have someone always watching out for me and prioritising me amidst all schedules. However, it would have been great if I had a couple of more years, perhaps the whole lifetime to spend with her. Twenty long years felt just like yesterday. Now even if I long for her precious company, I would never get it as there would be no one on the other end to reciprocate that feeling. There would be no one to comfort me at my lows, to appreciate me at my highs and be extremely exhilarated at my success and treat it as one's own. The physical intimacy, the sense of touch and all other humane forms of affection and warmth will indeed disappear in the dark. Her presence will be missed and there would forever be emptiness- a sort of void that can never be refilled because she was irreplaceable.

Being a doctor by profession, she was naturally empathetic and caring. She was bold, possessing a confident outlook towards her life and job as a whole. On the inside, she was an extremely emotional and sentimental person who valued the complexity and importance of human relationships and made every efforts possible to hold onto them. We often complain about the various adversities of our busy life and give a bucket-load of excuses for not being able to devote time for our family and our loved ones, notwithstanding the fact that time is fleeting. Time does not wait for our bantering to end. We fail to live within the moment, spend time with the people we prioritise and make memories worthy of remembrance. This in turn gives us guilt in the future, a form of regret from which we cannot escape. We think we could have reached great heights and achieved unbelievable records had it not been for our procrastinating self. We blame our destiny, luck and our surroundings for our misfortune, overlooking our complacent selves lacking vigour. Mummum however, was completely different than most people. She lived within the moment, understanding the very common notion of 'time once gone can never come back'. She did not believe in the power of fate and destiny, rather completely devoted herself to her work because according to her 'work was worship'. Rightfully so, it is our permanent allegiance and pure devotion towards our work that can help us gain immense fame, respect, reputation and the love of thousands of such people who are in dire need of our help. Through her profession and philanthropic works, she not only aided millions of people but also influenced many, perhaps an entire generation. It is both her work and her charming persona that made people adore her, genuinely appreciate her and have a profound sense of respect for her. This made us extremely proud because it never occurred in our minds that so many people other than us would love her as much as we do and mourn with us over this sudden misfortune. She was not only a role model of mine but also of plenty others.

Finally, I believe that even in this sombre ambience, in the midst of chaos, loss and grief, there is still a ray of hope. Death surely marks the end of an era but it also paves way for the beginning of one. The physical aspect of life- the flesh and bones get destroyed into fragments and returns to the universe from where everything started. But it is the metaphysical part of life, the achievements, works and legacy of a person that remains behind as footprints to be followed by those that remain. According to the laws of conservation of energy, "Energy can neither be created nor destroyed but gets converted form one form to another". Therefore Mummum's energy and presence can never be erased. It can be felt in every nook and corner of our house and every other place she has blessed her presence with. Her legacy, character, passion and dedication towards her profession will continue to serve as a source of inspiration for generations to come. So the most we can do right now is to imbibe and incorporate those good virtues within us and become a better version of ourselves. We as humans have great potential within us to not only strive for excellence but also serve those who are in need. Few good deeds can bring big changes. It is true that she had very little time and left us too soon but it is what she achieved within this brief timeframe that carved a mark in all our lives. Time is indeed momentary and brings unwanted changes in all our lives but it is what we make out of it that matters the most. If life is as futile as a blank page, then it is up to us to carve a whole meaning out of it and make it fruitful. It is we, the humans, who can make a change and augment the progress of mankind, thus opening doors for further exploration of all those unknown and unanswered questions.

A Preface From the Author's Fiance

It was exactly 6 in the morning when heard my mom knocking at the door. I woke up suddenly hearing the knock and from getting up to walking till the door, I had only one thing on my mind. I had changed the ATM pin for one of the cards which my dad was carry along with him, as he went to help Agniva's father on the way to bring back Aunty, his Maa. He went to Siliguri to help uncle and they were bringing her back. I was waiting for her back at home. I was waiting to talk to her eagerly.

Just the night before, as we were going to sleep, my fiance and me planned how we were going to meet each other before going and meeting Aunty, as she would be in Kolkata by next morning. How things change!

I was still walking towards the door. I thought my Baba had called to ask me to the new pin for the card that he might have forgotten. May be he needed to take out some cash. Maybe they reached Kolkata with Aunty. Maybe Papa just needed to speak to me. It was exactly 6 am.

As I opened the door I felt a numbing sensation grow inside me. I saw my mom stand outside, almost thawed from the inside. There was a moment of silence and then all hell broke loose. She looked at me and she broke down.

"Babu... Aunty nei. Aunty ar nei Babu..." (My child. Aunty is no more. She is gone)

And the silence only grew deeper...

Introducing
Dr. Rita Barai

*Act 1 scene 1: enter mom, my Maa,
my world, my universe!*

Maa was there, downstairs, in the garage, right next to her blue scooty, feeding the dogs some left over roti from the morning, while the dogs, Tingling, Light-Brownie, Biskittie, LeBrou and Blackie (names determined by their fur colours) flocked her from every side. I walked into the garage to meet her, greet her and talk to her, as she came back from her long day at her workplace, a hospital nearby.

She smelled like a hospital chemist shop and that pungent smell was a characteristic of her entering home. And just as I was about to feed a Chappati to Tingling, everything suddenly turned to black.

My eyes had opened. I was in Gurgaon. I was not home. There was no Maa around me. All those furry bundles of joy were not around me. I was alone, on my bed and as I kept looking at the ceiling, as it slowly kept turning. Time kept flowing, as it did four and a half billion years back when Gaia came into existence for the first time. Time kept flowing, like it will in another four and a half billion years from now when probably our personal star, the Sun would be busy preparing to start getting much bigger, in order for it to turn into a red giant and eat all the rocky planets. Time does not stop!

Relief is a word which people generally don't associate with death; death of a loved one, specifically. Some deaths bring relief, relief to them, the departed ones and relief to the family that eye witnessed their suffering.

What is life? How do we know something or someone is alive? How do we know what is life and death? Why does human society have so many rituals associated with life and death, while animals don't? Is this what the cognitive revolution entails for humans? What is mind? What is the brain? Do we have enough understanding of the husk we live in? Do we understand the basics of what we call to be alive? Do we know if what we feel at any point in time are by-products from the massive infrastructure of language and society or if they are actually what we think they are? Are emotions real or just careful chemistry? Is death the end of a life or just a simple chemical and physical change? Is death just the law of conservation of energy[26] being observed in the human realm?

There are so many questions I ask; rather keep asking. I have answers to many but I still euphemise those answers

---

[26] Law of conservation of energy – A law first proposed by Émilie du Châtelet. It states that energy can neither be created or destroyed. Energy can only be transformed from one form to another.

because I'm not happy with the truth. I'm not happy with the empirical and rational[27] answers.

I would rather be calmed and consoled with the societal, traditional and cultural answers because that's what brought peace to millions of humans. But will I be satisfied with those?

A book, specifically one written to read like a novel, generally doesn't contain research questions. But these questions say a lot about the way I was brought up. I was taught to question.

I was taught to understand the underpinnings, rather than look at the outcome and get devastated.

I was taught to question and be empowered with knowledge rather than blindly justify everything with archetypal knowledge. I was taught to examine and then believe anything I wanted to. I was allowed to make choices and I was given freedom of thought. Nonetheless, nothing prepared me for what happened on 22 March 2022.

---

[27] Rational – a specific way of thinking which involves past experience entailed with logic and the tendency to find reason and sense beyond the use of empiricism. It is used in research and life.

Day Zero – Predestination

The day my life changed forever

Maa will never speak again. Maa will never love me again, holding me in her arms. I'll never come back home to her shouting at the dogs or her calmly watering the beautiful plants she had cultured for years to have them bloom.

She will never ask me to trim my hair or not wear the paradigmatic[28] combination which she feels like is an absolute syntagmatic[29] mess.

She will never come back. When I last met her and she was not happy about me leaving home for my occupation, I didn't know that was the last time I would see her in my life.

---

[28] According to Ferdinand de Saussure, it means choices.

[29] According to Ferdinand de Saussure, syntagms are the rules that guide us. In this sentence, it just means rule or law.

Granted I had seen her after that over WhatsApp video calls but that was the last time I held her.

The smell of formalin on her cloths when she returned from the hospital and the way the street Indies would flock to her when she would return home, spoke a lot about her nature and the way she was with the world around her.

I mean how can the one who is absolutely responsible for who I am, not exist. The sixth element makes up a lot of our body. When we are made, it's just a genius of alchemy, the real one, we generally refer to as sex with a mix of lot of luck, practise and orgasms. In my opinion (feel free to argue with me) when we die, we just stop being ourselves.

We un-identify ourselves with the notion of self and stop being mindful or rather, stop all cognitive functions of the brain. The world around us learns to unlearn the habits we had, the things that made us what we are, the people who were the closest to them and what they stood for.

What they can never unlearn, if someone like me exists i.e. someone who loved them and loves them more than anything else is that they will never be forgotten.

They can be immortalised in spite of their de-existence in their sesto elementary[30] form. They can live on through our associations in memory, stories and family.

When someone dies, all their aspirations, dreams, visions and future dies with them.

Death is a strange equaliser which is as such, such a bitter yet dangerously strong stench which arises out of a gutter when a carcass rots and yet in some ways, it's beautiful yet honest; true. Death, or the notion of de-existence just takes you out of existence.

The corporal body, the spirit, the alpha the omega and the zodiac are all manifestations of our beliefs in what we call alive.

When Maa died, I wished for a miracle. I wished that suddenly she would wake up from that deep cold slumber and would shout out at me and say, "Ki korchish eta. Oporey giye bosh" (what the hell are you doing? Go upstairs). I sincerely wished on a miracle and wanted her to be alive.

When I was on the flight from 7 to 9 am, Maa was in a state of constant flux.

---

[30] Sesto elemento – a reference to Lamborghini's famous supercar. Here it just refers to Carbon, the sixth element in the periodic table.

When dad sounded absolutely broken at 6am before my flight I knew the flux was changing towards oblivion but I grit my teeth and I wanted to believe she would wake up again. I would hear her again, I thought. I didn't.

When I was on the flight, Maa was the Schrodinger's[31] cat. She was neither dead nor alive. My phone was off and until I got the news or confirmation that her cognitive being has suddenly stopped existing, she would neither be alive or dead. I had the possibility of believing in both but I still inclined on the fact that she was gone. It's no sixth sense, it's just intuition. I knew she was gone.

Maa was more than a backbone to me. Yes, I'm made up of her. My whole body was made by Maa. She made me who I am and she made me what I am. I got most of my behavioural aspects from her. I'm a feminist because she was one; not one of those Femi Nazis but a true blood

---

[31] Schrodinger's cat - In quantum mechanics, Schrödinger's cat is a thought experiment that outlines a paradox of quantum superposition. In the experiment, a speculative cat might be viewed as all the while both alive and dead because of its destiny being connected to an arbitrary subatomic occasion that could conceivably happen. This thought experiment test concocted by physicist Erwin Schrödinger in 1935, in a conversation with Albert Einstein, to delineate what Schrödinger saw as the issues of the Copenhagen understanding of quantum mechanics. The situation is many times included in hypothetical conversations of the understandings of quantum mechanics, especially in circumstances including the estimation issue.

feminist who believed in the truth, honest just outcome. She was just and true. Sometimes so honest that it pricked me; me who lies at times to get things my way. At times I'm radically honest and that's when I'm her son.

Think about it this way. My Maa is no more but am I not her? Well, obviously our Aadhar cards say otherwise but think about it again. I'm literally made inside her. So if the off springs live on, do the birthers[32] actually die? No!

Correct me if I'm wrong.

If she dies, she lives on through me, her son, her DNA, her body, her flesh, a huge part of her habits and largely her. She lives on through what I am and I will never let her die.

Real death occurs when people forget people, when they are not remembered anymore, when they don't exist anymore in memories, in associations and in conversations. Maa you'll always remain in my conversations.

I keep her WhatsApp chat alive, just so that I can text her once in a while and pretend like she is still here. Baba

---

[32] Birthers – a term the author has created to represent all mothers who give birth and yet remain mostly unappreciated. Mothers all over the world need to be appreciated. When they give birth, birthdays of their children need to be celebrated for them, not the children. Be it any gender, the child identifies with, every mother's months of toil to have given birth to their progeny, needs to be appreciated, more than it gets praise, now!

keeps using Maa's phone, talks to her friends from her phone as days progress. It feels so weird and eerie when Baba texts me from her phone but at the same time that familiar face, that celestial smile and that name 'Maa' in my notification suddenly makes me feel so calm and yet cold. It feels outright criminal even thinking about trying to delete Maa's contact, as if the bit of her that is left would be gone if I deleted her contact. I keep her chat alive so that I get some semblance of hope in such desperate times. And alas! She's giving me hope even on death!

Just the last time I saw her, she was this bundle of joy, joyous at the sight of her son hugging her and holding her tight. She could not see me before she died. She couldn't hug me, one last time. She couldn't hear me console her or scold her for her follies anymore. The sign relationship between the concept of motherhood and the phonemes which make up the word would now be an awkward and unfortunate topic for me. While life would go on, I would have to live with her memories, stumbling into smalls fragments of memory while I cruise through every part of life, alone, without my Maa.

One of the biggest reasons I never had a lot of friends is because I have such amazing parents. Correction ... I have such an amazing parent. Maa is gone. But she was the best part of me. With her gone, a part of me is permanently gone. While I really regret that she isn't here anymore and that makes me nauseous, I know that she is someone I can never forget. Forgetting is far off; I can't stop thinking about her. I had this habit of asking everything from her and running everything through her, the moment I had to decide. She always made me decide on my own and make judicious decisions but I still couldn't hold ground on my decisions alone. Seems like, now, I have been forced to make my decisions on my own.

Maa loved flowers, specially the yellow kind. She loved playing with beautiful yellow flowers and used to send me all the different flowers she had cultivated in her beautiful terrace garden, maintained and half made by dad. I would wake up in the morning to see her water the plants.

I remember the days I would leave home, back for work, away from home. She would be so damn sad but she would still water the plants. Every other day I woke up late but on those days I woke up early to accompany Maa at the terrace, while she watered the plants. It wasn't to my taste but I wanted to accompany her there. I just wanted to be with her. Well, guess I can't anymore. Every passing moment I keep living without her, is every moment I realise she's not here anymore.

It all feels like a weird dream like it never happened at all. Feeling is believing and somehow my hands still feel her warmth, in spite of the stark lack of it. I am not sure if I'm pretending to believe in the untrue or if I'm just denying what the truth is but what is true is that like every other crab[33], it's very difficult for me to let go.

---

[33] Crab – crab or the Cancerian astrological sign dwellers are supposed to grab onto memories, people and places. They do not let go easily. That is what the belief is. The author does not

When we were young, we used to dream about so many fictions come true and we used to salivate to such dreams. Maybe today, just today I want to grow young for once and go back to when I still didn't associate a few signifiers to signifieds. I would also love for time travel to be true. What I would not do to see her again! If there is time travel in the future and if anybody is reading this, probably dropping by at my room on 22nd March at 17:37pm would be great. A sign would be probably okay. I don't know; whatever!

Youth begets wisdom as time proceeds and enters the realm of infinite adulthood. Some of us, are not ready for adulthood. I guess, the burdens of adulthood have a reputation, that proceeds them. Sometimes, I think, everyone wants to be a kid again, when everything can be turned into a make believe fiction and concepts like existent or non-existent are just concepts; not things to be tensed about. Would circumstances be different had they visited my place, instead of they being at another place. Would she being with me have changed the outcome of 22 March?

How would things be different and would things be different had she never gone there and visited me? Probably she would still be here with me and I head first in her lap waiting for her to massage my head. That reminds me how she used to unendingly fan a copybook,

---

believe that apparent position of the stars can affect human behavior and personality though.

way back when I was very young. Load sheddings would never make me afraid because

I knew Maa would be there to fan the heat away from the room. She would shoo away the mosquitos and remove all the discomfort. I regret not being able to do that for her when she needed me the most. I regret not being there with her, when she needed her son the most. I will have to live with that now. I will never get rid of that guilt now. I wish I had arrived a couple of days earlier and spent some time with her. I wish she was here.

Day Zero – Memories of a Past Life

The other side of the day

Dad has been playing her recitations on repeat and I can't but ignore that beautiful, melodious voice anymore. It's like she's speaking right into my ear. It's like she's speaking to me. Her voice stings. It stings like a beautiful thorn to my ear now. Nothing is permanent. That's what she was reciting. That's what dad is playing back. No one stays forever and no one remains in this mortal realm forever. Her words seem proof of such transience. Fragile, broken, stupid life! I wish I could just ask papa to stop playing back her recordings but his silent tears and swollen face, from not having slept the last few nights, because he was there with Maa while I wasn't, tell a different story and I cannot but ask him to stop. He blames himself for not having done enough to have saved her. I don't blame him. I never will. He did a lot. I know that. But she gave us all a lesson. A life lesson on enduring life. Think about it; they fell in love long time back and after like around 40 odd years dad just has to accept the fact that she is no more. I mean she doesn't exist anymore. She is just another figment of imagination, if not anything else. How can I expect him to be fine when I can't accept her absence? Her absence is not transient though.

Catharsis with Maa

How I wish, she would suddenly open the doors of my room and then sit down by my side, open her phone, scroll through Facebook or watch a video on birds, a video on plants and then talk to me endlessly for hours. How I wish, she would be here with us! She was the best part of us! How I wish she would speak again! How I wish she would exist again!

Let's go back a couple of years when I was sleeping on the bed, inside the mosquito net and Maa came, crept inside, kissed my forehead and told me," Tatai, boromama ar nei". (Tatai, your maternal uncle is no more). I liked him a lot and was instantly in tears when I heard this. Maa held me tight and told me, time heals everything. I wish to go back to then, when it was Maa who broke the bad news to me, instead of being the one who would be the bad news. I wish she was alive.

I used to get irritated at Maa for not paying attention to the actual landscape of the place. She would go bonkers on the flora and fauna of the place, specifically flowers and birds; the others being selectively removed from existence. I wish I could still be irritated with her. I really wish.

Has Tuli accepted it? She seems to be in a reality loop where she isn't happy to accept the facts, and for the right reasons. I don't accept too. I guess, that's why she and I both don't want big pics of Maa everywhere with overbearing garlands on them. Seeing those would be like a reality icebreaker, poking a finger into our eyes letting us know that she is really gone. Like, it is not needed at all. Or maybe it is. Is it?

Tua feels very lonely. Mummum (Maa and Tua used to call each other Mummum) couldn't kiss her one last time in the ICU, since she was under dialysis. Tua might be my uncle's daughter but she has never behaved or felt like that. I've always loved her like my sister and so did Maa. She lost Maa too and the way she held me and cried this morning, tells me how much she has lost.

No one told me anything in the morning. I just knew she was no more. When I landed my uncle just told me," We are returning." I realised what that meant and even if I wanted to break down and cry and cry and cry, I could not. I was frozen!

Truth be told, I didn't want to see Maa in the way she was in the morning. It doesn't make a difference though. Today's image of Maa will remain in my mind forever as just the day she didn't smile and didn't kiss me and didn't hold me tight when I did the same to her and I'll not blame her for that. Let me reiterate, once again, that I am what I am because this is what she has raised me to be. All of you know me, probably have some or the other kind of feelings towards (or against) me because of the fact that she's my Maa (ah dad! Trust me you played a very important role all along and now you have to play both Maa and baba...sorry! You must).

There are a lots of people in the house now, and as many people calling us over telephones. I somehow want to cocoon inside a covering and sleep, till I can wake up from this bad dream. April will never come again. April was when Maa said she will come see me. She never will, again and April will never come again.

Catharsis with Maa

The number of people who cry when you are gone is a big denominator of how good you've lived your life. There is no life after death, or, at least that is what I believe. There is no life before life, that is also what I believe. But Maa was someone special. When she was lying there lifeless, smiling at all of us, from a probable heaven, every bloody one was crying. Everyone was in shreds while she silently escaped all of us. I've never seen so many people in tears for a doctor. Yes, she's been the saviour for so many, makes one think that the saviour will be saved by many. But then Jesus probably would be alive now. Probably, Galileo would be alive, when he spoke sense as well. Who knows!

Asking questions is something most people avoid because they are not happy with getting asked questions, when they ask questions. Maa taught me to be reliable and valid, in the sense of research. She taught me to question, she taught me to reconfigure my outlook, relook, requestion and keep questioning what's happening around us, no matter how 'normal' they seem to us. She taught me to be vigilant, just and honest.

Baba keeps on showing me the last pic, he clicked of Maa. He's not happy with the diagnosis which Maa got. He's not happy with the hospital or their prognosis. Maa might have been here, had it not been for the wrong prognosis. I want baba to be happy with her last picture. I want baba to not live in the past, not be reminded of Maa's lifeless cold body lying in front of him, while he cried in vain, trying to bring her back, wishing she would wake up and come back to life. She didn't. Baba still keeps crying and smiling. He's inconsolable but he pretends to have a very hard outer shell. He pretends to be strong while I know how much he's hurt.

No one will ever bother me saying," Tatai, kalyani te nursery te niye chol plz" (Tatai please take me to the plant nursery in Kalyani). She and I used to go to get saplings which are now part of her amazing terrace garden. She used to pick up saplings, trees, roots, seeds, barks and so on and so forth. When she would come back from a trip, her bag would be no better than rug collector's. She would literally pick up whatever she wanted to pick up. God she was irritating at times, when she would literally sneak up on plants and pick them up like a seasoned klepto but God, she was cute.

I'll sleep on the same pillows when I'm home but I'll never sleep next to you with your warm breath on my forehead Maa. The smell of your neck when I held you tight and imagined myself to be the little tata, you always loved so much. You would have definitely held me so tight, consoled me, told me things would be okay if you saw me the way I'm now; broken; broken so much that it seems like with you a part of me died today.

Maa, your presence was everywhere in my life. From the minutest of things to the most major things, everything reminds me of you. The smallest of odours, the littlest of flowers, the beautiful clouds, every plant, every bird reminds me of you; the over enthusiastic birdwatcher gardener. I love you Maa. I still can't believe you're gone.

Catharsis with Maa

Relief is a term no one would associate with death but I do now. Maa was in a lot of pain. Last evening was the last time I spoke to her, forever but it was the worst time I spoke to her. Her voice sounded so different, portraying the kind of pain she was undergoing. It killed me inside to have heard her like that. I regret the fact that she along with our whole family was on a trip and I couldn't talk to them, the last few days she existed. I missed her in the mornings, when I generally used to call her but I refrained from calling her when she was on a vacation. Looks like I'll live with that regret forever. I miss her already, a hell lot. Probably in a couple of day the pain will lessen and the blemishes will stop bleeding.

Maa was so busy treating others that we forgot to stop and check her and find out what was wrong with her. No one stopped till she stopped forever. No one battered an eyelid till she was busy distributing favours, medicines and smiles.

Everybody got so used to her being the hashira (pillar) in the family that her not being here is like a magnanimous black hole. Everybody's first stop into treatment in the family would be Maa or Boudi (sister in law) or Jemma (elder aunty) or Mummum (Tua called her this and previously when I was young I called her this), Rita (what elders called her). Her being gone has created a hole so deep, that it smiles and smirks on Kola Super Bore hole.

I want to wake up tomorrow morning and see Maa which I know I will not and that breaks me so bad. Every time I came back home, I'd sleep right next to her, while dad would sleep in another room. Maa would talk to me till late hours, asking me things and questions about other things. She used to ask me if I remember chewing on her hair, making her lose a lot of hair and in turn going to sleep, only by the virtue of doing it. She used to ask me whether I remember her applying powder to me everywhere. I'll never get back those conversations. I'll never get back Maa.

There's this picture of Maa and me where I'm on her lap and she has my hand held. We are feeding something to Mami (My younger Mama's wife – the brother closest to Maa in terms of age) on the day of her wedding. It looks so beautiful. I don't know, I just got reminded. it certainly, somehow cements the idea of motherhood for me; handholding, caring, loving, guiding, philosophising and friend. She was everything to me.

At some point in time, I really started wishing that a black hole would suddenly engulf me, the earth and everything or maybe suddenly, Maa would be restored and replaced with me. I really wished that suddenly the programmer and developer responsible for coding the simulation, would wake up and realise it was a bug; restore Maa and then relaunch the program and voila, tomorrow morning, everything would be perfect.

When everyone was touching her, I suddenly felt like her hand moved. I suddenly felt like she was looking at me, hating the fact that I was helplessly waiting for a miracle, crying my heart out while I was grabbing her hand but this time she didn't hold me back. Her hands were cold and she was not there. Once, just once I thought she'll wake

Catharsis with Maa

up and tell us all it was a big fat planned joke and then tell us all to be merry.

Maa loved to moisturise herself and along with that, anyone who would be around her, specifically me and Tua. She would literally bathe me in moisturiser. I would hide my hands, my legs, my face from her. Now I want to play hide and seek again, with Maa. Maa where are you?

When I would be home and I would wake up around 7 am, long after Maa's wake up time at 6am, when she woke up to talk to her green buddies, I would go to the staircase and shout,"Maaaaaa" and wait for her response. Depending on where she responded from, I would either head to the terrace or downstairs. Sometimes I would just request her to call me once the milkman delivered that day's milk and I would sleep another 30 mins. I regret sleeping and not spending more time with her. I regret not spending more time with her. At the rarest of times when I would wake up and head to the terrace, I would walk like a cat. I would silently go to the terrace and go stand behind her, only for her to realise a few mins later. She would burst out into laughter and call me a cat. No one will do that anymore. I won't ever do that anymore. I suddenly grew up from being her son, to just another adult who keeps on cribbing about life. I would never be able to wake up beside her anymore, feel her tangled hair, all over my arms, making me feel itchy or listen to her croaky voice in the morning trying to wake me up. Sometimes she would call me from the terrace to show me a rare bird, a Phalaenopsis, maybe a Vanda or maybe just the beautiful sky. Who will show me those now? My chat with Maa is filled with birds, seeds, plants and skies. She loved to share with me and baba. We have an empty space, we can't fill for each other. We weren't exactly ready for this...

Every time I would come back to my workplace for another 2 or 3 months, Maa would give me an exhaustive packet of medicines for contingencies. I still have the collection from the last 3 times. Those are Maa's last supplies to me. I'll never consult a doctor that easily, as I did with Maa, nor will we, as a family, ever get medical supplies, nor will we get medicine suggestions. I'll never take advantage of the fact that Maa would always take care of me. I couldn't take care of her. She died not knowing what intensive care from children would be, at old age.

She always wanted to see the Northern lights[34]. This is a regret I would always live with. Right now, I don't even want to plan about going to somewhere to ever see it, like ever. It was her dream. I wanted to see it with her and dad. Now it will always be a fairy tale, that could have been.

---

[34] Northern Lights – Aurora Borealis – a form of lightning, also called slow lightning where the sky lights in various colours due to the interaction of charged particles from the sun with the magnetization of the poles.

Day 1

The illusion of control

Baba was strong in the morning when people were around. He smiled at everyone and took everyone's call. I kind of wrapped myself in a cocoon and just avoided calls altogether. I just couldn't speak. I was a bit surprised to see him so calm and composed. It gave me a lot of strength. At night, he was inconsolable. He kept on crying. I held him tight. Not that I don't love him, but I just imagined I was holding Maa, like I always did. Don't get me wrong. I and dad are really close but I never saw him this vulnerable. He put up a facade all day long, to make sure everyone doesn't keep on lecturing him. But at night, he was at his lowest. He set an alarm at 4.45am, just so that he can wake up and think about Maa. It was the time when she finally left her corporal body and entered the ethereal. It was the time she died. I want to be there for baba and everyone else but I feel broken; terribly broken. I feel like a cab without wheels trying to ferry passengers for free.

Last afternoon when Maa's still, cold body was here and I walked into that room, I opened Schrodinger's box. Finally. Till then she was not dead for me. She was neither alive nor dead. I looked carefully to check whether it was her and suddenly reality hit me so hard. I saw her beautiful face, eyes closed, looking as if she's sleeping. Yes she was sleeping, peacefully, oblivious of all pains, oblivious of the fact that her son was broken inside to see her like that and was kissing her cold dead cheeks goodbye, one last time, crying inconsolably because Maa would never wake up and kiss me back. The first thing I noticed and felt was how cold her body was and I just wanted to not touch her anymore. I just wanted her body to feel warm again. Somehow I realised, she was gone. I've seen series and soaps where doctors announce the time of death. I wonder what they said when Maa passed away. I wonder what they said because she was in pain, not being able to see her closest loved ones, one last time. I wonder what she felt like in her last moments, what she thought, who she wanted to hold, one last time and how much she cried. I miss you Maa.

One day has passed since Maa left us and I sincerely want to admit that I still wish I would replace her instead. I wish that I would be the one gone, while she would be here. But then, she would be in extreme pain, since she loved me so much. But nonetheless, she would be alive, in pain. When my eyes opened today, I really wished I never woke up and I really wished I woke up to a bad dream. There was a terrible calm today.

When we came back after Maa's cremation, I came upstairs, crept into my bed and silently cried, while Tuli looked into my eyes, tried to console me and broke into fits of inconsolable tears herself. I didn't know if I had to console her or stop myself. I was so confused. One thing

I dreaded to do was to open the room in which Maa and baba stayed. I knew I was sweaty after the whole day but that was the last day I touched Maa. At the back of my mind, I didn't want to change but I realised, I must. While I was standing at the washroom, trying to fill the bucket with water, I slowly crept out of the washroom and my hands were already on the door knob of their room. Before knowing anything, I had turned the knob and I was inside the room. The room was lifeless, empty, the bed being filled with junk (Maa liked collecting a lot of junk and she also loved to keep her collections on the bed). Maa was not there but there were only memories. Up until I was 16 years old, we stayed in the room I stay in now and I have more memories there than in the new room. Nonetheless, I have so many memories of the new room. Maa getting ready for work, while I kept disturbing her. Before the age of digital money, I saw her hiding money in multiple places and she knew that I know where she hid them. I asked her why she didn't hide it from me, to which she said, "tor jonnoi toh korchi re gadha". (Imbecile, why hide from you. You are the future).

Last time Maa came to Gurgaon, I took her to Sohna view point and she loved that place. We went to multiple places and she loved it. She came to my university, she met my students, she met other colleagues of mine and she was happy with the place I was at. She loved the food from fuel zap but regret still remains. I couldn't take her to chai garam, or take her to another spot in Gurgaon I recently discovered, the leopard trail. She was my partner in crime. She even agreed to do a ladakh trip with me later on, as a pillion on my bike. Who will, now, do those Maa? I'm not strong Maa, definitely not as strong as you were. You were made of steel. You cried too but you were every bit, made of steel. You had nerves of steel. I cannot be strong like you. I am broken. I'm shattered Maa. I can only say I need you, but I know I'll never find your love, your care, your hugs, your kisses, your voice, your conversations again. Never!

I guess, I never saw so many people at once, when someone is being taken away for cremation. Maa was just another doctor but she definitely was loved by so many people. Thousands of people. In the end I could only see a heap of flowers and not Maa.

I keep on going back to my gallery, looking at Maa's photos. It gives me solace, it feels like she's not gone and then suddenly, bam, on the face, I remember the time when I saw her corporal body for the last time. Her lifeless body was on a wooden frame. That frame was slowly forwarded into the furnace and that was the last time I saw Maa. That was the last time I saw the body which gave birth to me, hugged me, fed me, loved me and grew me up. Then that body was burnt to a crisp till only a couple of bones remained. Flesh, skin, blood, hair...everything was burnt to a crisp. She died and her body was also turned into nothingness. Well, like Carl Sagan once said she actually, just like everyone else, was made of star stuff and she returned to it. Now she's one with the very flora and fauna she loved so much, as the very elements which travel long distances before meeting other elements which make sense for them to combine with.

When she was in the furnace, or rather when her body was in the furnace, she didn't feel the heat at all. She was already gone. I couldn't bear to see her body being forwarded into the furnace but I saw as her body was put into the furnace. I stood outside the crematorium looking at everything. I wrote a couple of pages down as well. Then I looked up at the sky and saw smoke leaving the distillation tower. That smoke was once the woman I held so close. That smoke was once a solid mass of nerve bundles that loved me unconditionally and would do anything for my happiness. That smoke was once the woman who saved so many people. That smoke was once the bundle of joy, dad fell in love with. That smoke was once filled with life, joy, happiness, glee and sang and danced at every opportunity she got. That smoke was once Maa.

No, I don't really have a huge friend circle. Maa and baba were my closest friends. Baba still is, but Maa isn't. While I regret that, probably she being there and me not needing anyone else for validation, friendship and guiding, made me such an unsocial mess. I never cared about relationships, specially friendships. I never had a push from behind to maintain friendships. Maa; I always called her, first thing in the morning after I sat in the cab or started to drive. I loved speaking to her. It was not a necessity but she was more like the reason I would stay awake all day. Speaking to her in the morning would keep me running all day long.

The illusion of control is a strange grandeur we invest in. Smart bands and smart watches, clinical visits, frequent diets and physical tests to check ailments are a rather normal picture of today, every day. People think they are in control and that's how they like to believe their reality. One moment of uncontrollability can shake up the whole dynamic of falsehood we call 'control'. Everybody in the family is still questioning if Maa would survive had they not gone on a trip, to a place which is very high. 15000 feet is not a joke and that can compromise body functioning. What we want to understand is why, she was perfect and laughed around, danced around when she was in Ladakh. Without going into the prognosis of the present situation and without thinking about how things could have been, here I am still questioning if Maa would still be here, had she visited me instead of visiting where she went. Maybe she would be here with me now, maybe not. Who knows! I wish she would still be here, with me. I want to feel her warm hands around my neck, her warm body when she used to hug me and then shrug me off, like saying, "Ah don't be a sissy. You'll be good".

When we used to sit for long hours, Maa used to tell me, "Onekdin gaan shonashni. Ekta gaan shonabi?" (You haven't sung for me in such a long time. Will you please sing for me?) I regret not being able to sing for her one last time. Maybe my singing would have kept her alive. Maybe me singing would have changed things. Maybe she just wanted to hear my voice, talking into her ears. Instead, she died alone, without anyone she loved. Baba says that the moment she was taken to the hospital on the ambulance stretcher, she had already collapsed and there was no voluntary breathing. She was already gone. But maybe if there was just an iota of sense left in her, she must have been torn on the inside knowing that, the doctor and the paramedics were busy in an attempt to save her life, while her only son was trying to board a flight to come see her and that her husband was downstairs, trying to admit her to a hospital. She died knowing that she would have to die with regrets. She would never see her husband again. She would never see her daughter again, never see her son again. Her consciousness faded before she could even think these things. She slowly drowned in an engulfing ocean of darkness, alone!

We think we have time, till time suddenly ceases to exist. Maa taught me that, the hard way. Even the last time I met her, I knew it for a fact that she was just 60 years old and she would definitely live another 30 years easily. She was fit as a race horse. Time ran out. Expectations and aspirations died with her. When I left home, I left knowing that I'll come back to see her again, soon and that I'll be in her arms again. Ah! I came back but she never hugged me back.

One reason I always came back was Maa. No matter what it was, I came back home to be in her presence. I loved her that much. Call me immature or anything but I just loved spending time with her. She was that important to me. I wonder about a few associations now. Will and should I still consider this my home knowing that Maa isn't here anymore. Do I still come back home, knowing that Maa will not be here to receive me at home or at the airport? Do I still come back home, knowing that dad will always look at my face and see Maa in my face. Do I still call this my home knowing that Maa is what I called home? Me and Tuli, we wanted to return home in another 5 years. We wanted to shift home because we wanted to be here with our old timers. Well, turns out Maa had other plans... Or did she? Going by her room, she wasn't ready herself. Even she thought she had time. She had planned so much. She had so many plans and she wanted so many things for our wedding. She was more excited than us.

The difficult part when grieving is that you have to have the guts to answer all questions that are fired towards you. A multitude of people will ask you a lot of things about the person you just lost and you just have to answer all those questions with a thump of lump stuck in your neck. You won't be allowed to swallow it or through it out. It's like that. You won't be able to cry because you don't consider them as close as you think they were and you won't be able to stay too strong, ie pretend to be strong because you just can't. I just lost Maa!

When I first got my PlayStation 3, Maa was so damn against it. She still believed in me playing outside and she knew I'd get bored with it in no time. Yes, in the long run I did get bored. I tried my best though, to get her into gaming. There was this game 'super rub a dub' where you had to control the joystick like a gyroscope to control a pool on screen. You had to control the flow of water to control ducks. I remember hand holding her and teaching her to play that game. I held her hands and almost irritatingly taught her to play. She became really good at it towards the end. Nothing, I just remembered this.

Catharsis with Maa

When I was young, like say 10 years old, the film Stuart Little was released. I remember wanting to see the film. I threw such a big tantrum. She told me that we are not going and she was very strict about it. I insisted that we go but she just scolded me shut. I went upstairs and lied down, crying. She came upstairs and asked me to come with her. I sat behind her on her scooty and we went out. I was not sure where we were headed but then eventually I realised what was happening. We were headed to the venue of the film and I knew it. In spite of knowing it I asked Maa where we were headed, to which she said, "You'll see Tatai". We watched that film that day. Maa knew how to make me happy, consistently. I didn't do much to make her happy except for being with her, which I loved doing. She was the one I was willing to do everything for, like she did for me, unconditionally, for such a long time.

Baba keeps responding to a lot of texts. People have been texting him, calling him. He's been putting up with the society. He's been putting up with appearances, conversations and he's been gritting his teeth, answering everything with a smile. I don't know exactly, how to console him except for doing everything I did with Maa. Last night I held him like I always held Maa. He said he was not Maa and he can never be and he felt so bad for that. He kept crying. I told him that I don't care and that it didn't matter. I would still take him to be my Maa and dad, now onwards. I need him. So does he.

Yesterday, when I sat in the flight, my whole life flashed before my eyes. I could see death in the eyes and talk to the God of death, if they existed. I felt like I died. I felt out of breath and extremely nauseated. My ears closed and I could not hear for almost 20 mins in between. These things never happened to me before. I don't know what happened. It was almost like a part of me was being cut away from me. I almost puked. I felt weak and my stomach behaved in ways, I had not experienced before. At that point in time, I still didn't know Maa was gone, at least not officially. But that's when I guess my body realised it. I didn't believe it till I saw her still cold body and touched her lifeless body. I didn't realise she was gone before her lifeless body was inside that red hot furnace and the door slowly closed while I saw her for the last time. But long before she was actually gone, while I sat there with my eyes closed, silently crying under the hankey I used to cover my face, I realised Maa was gone. I realised it because at that point in time nothing else mattered. It didn't matter if the flight crashed. It didn't matter if the world didn't exist. My world had suddenly stopped to exist. At that point in time, Maa had stopped to exist.

Every bit of me wants you to come back. But you'll never come back. I saw your body burn and then I picked through your ashes and poured holy water on it. Then we threw those ashes in the Ganges. I know you're gone. But what if you're not? What if you're still reading what I'm writing here? Rationalism doesn't exist for me anymore, I guess. I'd rather be happy with some empirical proof that you still exist but you don't, do you?

Catharsis with Maa

Last night baba wanted to set an alarm at 4.45 am. He didn't wake up because he couldn't sleep for the last 4 nights. He had to take care of Maa. He did so much. His whole body was seriously tired. I played with his hair and massaged his back till he slept and only then did I sleep. At 4.45am, the alarm went off but baba didn't wake up. I did. I woke up to realise that exactly 24 hours back, Maa was desperately fighting for her life, trying to stay conscious, trying to think of dreaming to meet us all, one last time before oblivion rubbed away her consciousness. She tried. I know. I broke down again. I cried till I couldn't breathe. I saw tua and baba sleeping. I silenced the phone, kept it beside baba and buried my face in the pillow. Maa didn't come and pick me up, scold me for being too weak or ask me to get up.

Long-time back, my first girlfriend came to visit me here, from Bangalore, where she was. I have always been bad at goodbyes and when she was leaving, after staying here for a week, I was sad. I was about to cry when Maa suddenly looked at me and gestured to me to be strong and smiled at me. I wish she can, from somewhere, send me a sign, tell me she's still here, in spirit, if that's a thing. I wish she could sincerely help me with this goodbye. I just wish.

When I was in school, Maa was posted in Bansberia, at a public health centre. She used to ride on her Bajaj sunny at that time. Our school used to get over at 3.15 pm and she used to time her return home, such that she would be able to pick me up. Most days, I would return with her, sitting behind her and holding her. I would be able to smell sweat, perfume and the odd smell of all things hospital on her. I still remember that smell. I would recognise that smell any day.

When we came back from the burning ghat, at first I kept my cloths in the laundry bag but then after a pause, I realised those were the last cloths in which I hugged Maa, no matter how lifeless she was when I did so. I took them out of the laundry bag and put them in a polythene and then stored them safely. This is something money can never buy. Sentimentalism is for fools but I would like to keep this piece of her, intact, with me, till I can somehow learn to live with the fact that Maa is gone.

Day 2

The nights are when it's the most difficult

It's been 2 days that Maa has left us. I didn't cry when I woke up but I'm just frozen. I couldn't do anything at all. I am just frozen and I cannot move. I looked to the side once again and imagined Maa sleeping peacefully while I looked into her hair but she was not there. Baba already woke up and went upstairs to care for their other children, the plants. This was something Maa and baba made in the last 2 years. They spend a lot of time and money on these plants. They have thrived. Baba thinks Maa is alive through the plants. These plants need to survive and their survival is of utmost importance. He lost her soul mate but he will take care of these plants to let Maa live thorough them.

I don't exactly remember what happened with the pics of Kashmir. I had given the pics of Kashmir to Maa but I cannot find them anymore. Maa won't click pics anymore. She took the Nikon P900 camera to Kashmir. Her last clicked pics were in it. I don't think I would be able to use that camera anymore. Maa loved clicking pics. She won't anymore. Kashmir album had so much variety. She clicked so many beautiful flowers and birds. The lakes looked beautiful while she was so happy in the snow. So happy! I feel guilty for not having saved the Kashmir pics properly and having given them to Maa. Who knew that in a couple of months I won't be able to simply send a WhatsApp to Maa and ask her, where the files are!

The room seems empty as of now. No matter how filled the rooms are, they will always be empty. Maa filled them with something, we lack consistently; happiness, laughter and glee. Waking up in the morning was not a task because I would wake up to her, either calling me downstairs to drink bournvita, or her calling me to the terrace to see a beautiful flower or bird. When I woke up and walked to the terrace yesterday, I walked slowly again, to the roof. I forgot Maa was not there. I walked and imagined when I would look into the orchid shade, Maa would be there again, with the water sprinkler in her hand, watering the plants. She wasn't. I thought I would suddenly see her there.

I want to hallucinate. I want to hallucinate a lot. I want to see her everywhere. I feel empty. Everywhere I'm sitting and doing anything alone, seems like a very difficult task. All day Tuli is here and there are other guests too but the moment everyone is gone, it feels like Maa is there. It's like I am imagining that she's standing right there the moment I open a door I can't see beyond, the moment I walk into a room or the moment I close and open my eyes. Please tell me this is a bad dream! Children have always dreamt of their parents leaving them but I think I've dreamt long enough. I don't want to dream this anymore. This pain is unbearable.

Catharsis with Maa

They say your emotions are best recollected in tranquillity. Wordsworth's[35] every word in poetry, was worth it. I've decided to pen down my feelings in the way I remember things. I'll probably publish it when I'm a bit better after venting out everything. Maa will stay alive through my prose. But I'm never tranquil and I'm either in extreme grief or I can't feel anything anymore. How do I write?

I always knock a door when I know someone's inside. This morning I knocked Maa and Baba's room once again. I forgot Maa won't be inside, probably organising things inside, while disorganizing another part of the room. Organizing and cleaning wasn't her strong suit but I always helped her with that. Trust me when I say she wasn't good at it. Trust me when I say, she still taught me to organize and for the few last years, I have been organizing things for her, for Tulika, for baba. Maa wasn't the best at it, but she made me so self-sufficient that she started to bank on me. I loved doing it for her. I'll probably never be able to do it for her again. Damn! That's denial. I'm still in denial.

Maa is just a bunch of memories, pictures, videos now. I'm being asked by everyone to send pics of Maa everywhere. How can I? Those were pics of my Maa. I don't want to send them Maa's pics. I don't want to. She was mine and mine only. Sharing her pics is like sharing

---

[35] William Wordsworth – one of the major names when it comes to the romantic movement.

her with everyone. She was my Maa. I can't help it. Now I'm stuck sorting through pics of Maa, trying to make sense, trying to make sure I find her best pics. It's an improbable yet, to be done, task. I don't know what to do.

Here I'm in the same room her lifeless body was, for the last time. Her eyes were covered with petals. Her hair was covered with flowers, her forehead smeared with vermillion and her body smeared in a strong sense of incense sticks. Personally I hated that. I buried my face in her hair, trying to smell her one last time. The whole room had this strong smell of death. Death smells like flowers and incense sticks. Tube roses, hibiscus and Tekoma[36] were all over her slightly bloated body. Damn! Her kidneys were such a bummer. Kaku silently plucked three orchids from her beautiful garden. He came and silently put three of those on Maa's forehead. I

looked at him and rebuked him saying that this was something Maa hated and he should not have plucked those. When I looked into his eyes, he was already in tears and he couldn't breathe. Baba took those flowers and put them in Maa's still hands. She held her flowers when she was in that final inferno. I still can't get myself to look straight at that room. I still can't sit and look at the room. I went inside that room to brave the circumstance but I still can't get myself to imagine how Maa's lifeless body was there, while hundreds of people came and saw her,

---

[36] Various kinds of flowers that grow at the author's house, even today

offered her flowers, offered her respect and love. If there's life after death, she must be smiling.

Mornings are practically much more easier than nights now. Nights are when you're not busy anymore and you have time to think. You're still getting used to the unlearning process. I keep smelling random things Maa touched and probably follow it up with a kiss to it. Sometimes I just sift through random things she used every day and then imagine her hands on mine. It gives me no strength. It just makes me sad. It makes me sick to the core but the smell of her skin just makes me feel sick yet complete. In those transient and momentary times, I feel like I still got to feel her. I know it's once again stupid but it's what it is.

I feel sick to the core. So many people have been calling us to attend these gatherings for Maa, that I'm practically tired. But coming to Chandannagore IMA[37] proved to me how much of an amazing angel she was. She was a social worker, a doctor, a philanthropist and an amazing woman. She was my Maa.

When I was young, I used to look at Maa with my puppy eyes and request her to take me to Chinsurah station. Maa used to get me dressed up, walk me to Gorosthan more and we would wait for a trekker. A trekker is a vehicle which looks like an SUV with no doors. It would to ferry

---

[37] IMA – the Indian Medical Association It is an association of all doctors in India, membership being voluntary.

people from the bus stand to the station. Maa used to sit me in the trekker and then we would go to the station, count around two to three trains and come back again. I loved looking at those magnificent beasts. They looked so complicated yet beautiful. Maa let me enjoy that. This evening I heard the sound of a train and I couldn't get myself to think of anything else except Maa. But then I suddenly remembered how Maa doesn't exist anymore.

I had gone to drop Tuli back home. When I left, I saw Maa's helmet in the garage. When I came back, I was alone in the garage and I picked up her helmet and smelled the inside of the helmet. I suddenly felt like I was kissing my Maa's head. It smelled like her sebum and her body. It was so comforting yet breaking apart at the same time. I couldn't help but imagine all those years she used to ferry me from place to place. I couldn't imagine that not happening again. Just a few months back when I was sick in the Covid-19 pandemic, Maa took me to the hospital for an RTPCR[38] Covid test and now I have to live with the fact that there's no Maa.

---

[38] RTPCR – Reverse transcription polymerase chain reaction; a process made much more famous during the Covid19 pandemic.

Day 3

The system failed her

It's been three days since Maa left us now. I don't know if it's getting easier to live life or I'm just getting used to living with the pain. Maa used to wake up in the morning, make sure we were all sleeping peacefully, tucked in all of us once again and then would go upstairs to her green children. This morning when I woke up, dad was faced the other way, towards Tua. I knew it was not Maa. By now, the expectations of her being there are steadily decreasing. But for once, I closed my eyes and imagined me running my hands on Maa's shoulders and hair. It gave me such relief. Baba held my hands, because he knew what I was doing and the dream was over!

I opened my eyes again this morning to a call Baba got from a distant family. "What do I say? She's not here because of the carelessness of corporate doctors! She was a doctor herself and she's always saved people. It's ironic how the angel who saved thousands could not be saved by thousands of people in one major corporate hospital in Siliguri. They didn't even consult her while she wanted to. They didn't even give her food at proper times. They didn't even care for her. They did 416 tests on her but they were yet to find the problem. She didn't give them time. They couldn't find out what exactly happened to her." Before baba could go on, I got up, ran out. I am honestly a bit tired of listening to how Maa died, by now. I want to remember how people loved her. I want to remember how she would play with me. I want to remember how she would play with children. I want to remember how, when she used to return, Tingling, Biskittie, Le Brew, Bagha, Blackie and the other furry kids used to literally gherao her and demand love. They knew she was one who would always be there for her. Last night Tingling and her gang entered our garage and I played with them for a couple of minutes but they were still looking for Maa. Maa used to come and feed them, always. I fed them but they were still looking for her. I told them that she will never come again. Don't know, if they got that but coincidentally Tingling looked at me, and eventually her waving tail stopped. She came straight to me while I was kneeling down to pat their warm furry bodies and hold their beautiful souls. Tingling slowly rubbed her head into my tummy and then looked at me, as if to say something. Then she left. Coincidentally, everyone else left as well. I know they will come back, and that no one will interpret this in the way I did, but somehow they seemed like they wanted to send a message. Empirical science begets the fact that we humans try and rationalise occurrences that have happened by trying to rationalise it with information that has been made available to us, after an incident and that is what I was doing. While I was reminded of this, I ran to Maa and Baba's room and opened it. I was angry that Maa was not there. I was angry that I couldn't see her sleeping there. I was angry that like before I couldn't ask her to wake up and come with me to the terrace. I was angry because her sleep was too deep and nothing would be able to wake her up.

When Alice died, Maa was sad for so many days. Maa loved Alice a lot. I loved Alice a lot. Alice was in coma, the last day before she died. She couldn't move, she couldn't look, she couldn't eat, she couldn't get up. She needed help with everything. The only thing that her body still had functioning was her involuntary body functions. We were so broken and I couldn't gather the strength to go inside the room, she was in. I was crying alone. She was my sister and Maa brought me up in exactly the same way. Maa never treated her like a dog. She never grew up in a family, that hated dogs. Maa used to feed us the same things. She used to adore both of us together. That night, Maa didn't come to sleep with us, nor did Alice. Maa knew that Alice might stop breathing at any time. Maa was there with Alice. In the morning around 5 am, Alice started to gasp for air. Maa shouted out to us. I was young and I blame myself for still not being aware that Maa was shouting and that I kept sleeping. Baba rushed downstairs to his wife and daughter. Maa told me later that the moment she held Alice in her arms, she stopped breathing as if she was waiting for Maa to hold her in her arms. Maa came upstairs while I was still sleeping and woke me up. She told me, "Alice ar nei" (Alice is no more). Tears rolled down my cheeks and I couldn't speak. She hugged me and asked me to come downstairs. I saw Alice's lifeless body. I knew Alice would no longer play with me, no longer chase me when I would hug Maa and no longer lick my face as if it was food. I loved her. She was gone. However, what I didn't know was that, Alice won't be here with me, when the woman we both loved more than ourselves, would suddenly, shockingly leave us all.

I have a strange aversion to incense sticks. Probably it's because I've never been religious, never loved doing rounds to temples, never have been appreciative about Gods and Goddesses and the only time I've ever smelled incense sticks were when I was at someone's death gathering or when I had to purchase them for Amma from a crowded shop. You see, my association with incense sticks started on the wrong foot. This morning when I smelled incense sticks at the terrace, I was suddenly teleported back to the sight of Maa's cold body. I tried hard to not fixate with that untowardly sight of everyone crying while Maa was there, still and not breathing but I did. This is going to take more time than I imagined it would. Nothing bothers me anymore. An ambulance rushing to the hospital, today's overcast sky making everything look gloomily beautiful, the beautiful flowers Baba is watering now, the birds chirping in the distance, the chicken being killed for being consumed at Sahil's shop downstairs or the wind slowly caressing my hair. Nothing matters...

If waiting for "acche din" in India was a pain, it will be excruciating for me to wait for hearing Maa's voice once again. It'll be difficult to wait for Godot knowing that Godot will never come. It'll be difficult to wait for the 'holud pakhi' from Cactus's famous song of the same name and it'll be impossible to go back to the same places I loved going to, without the presence of the woman who made it worthwhile. Maa will never come back again. Never!

Right around 6 pm, when I would be resting would be when Maa would video call me over WhatsApp every day. I would reach home around 4.30pm, hassle with the scrolling up of ritualistic social networks till 5.15 pm and then would probably go to sleep for a hour. I hated it when Maa called me around 6pm and she knew it and in spite of that she would call me to listen to me, talk to me and look at her son's face after a busy day. I would at times ignore her call and call her back around 6.40pm, when I would be up. I wish I never did that. I wish I never ignored her. I know she never felt like she was alone because I always was there for her, so was dad but I can't get rid of the feeling that I should have not ignored her. I feel guilty, very guilty for having done that. I can never do that again. Now, when, I'll come back from office, no one will call me; no one will ever ask me about my day and no one will ever wake me up from sleep. No one will love me the way she did.

Tua is a welcome change. She blasted into the room where I was working on the question papers. She was smirking at Kakima, saying that she doesn't need 1 litre of water, even in a day, let alone 3 hours at the college. She's a breath of fresh air. She takes after Maa. She's such a bright and beautiful soul, just like Maa. I was still working and just like Maa, she tapped my head and said, "Dada I'm going to the college" and just like I told Maa, I told her, "Come back safe and soon". Some people survive cancer, some people survived Chernobyl, some people like me have survived terrible road accidents with issues and stories to tell lifelong, some people have survived air crashed, some people have survived a lightning bolt, some people have survived extreme electrocution and active euthanasia on being sentenced to death, some people have survived hanging to death but Maa didn't survive pulmonary embolism with thrombosis. Maa couldn't. The system failed her. The system, consisting of flesh eating maggots ruining the freshness of medicinal treatments, the vultures waiting for every bit of money slipping through the frail hands of patients and the boa constrictors waiting to swallow honesty, fundamental rationalism and goodness of heart. Maa chided this system aside and helped everyone. In spite of multiple threats to her well-being, being in this very system, she has been survived by thousands of people she helped survive, through this failing system. But this system failed her...

Beautiful Lies

*11 years back, through
Maa's eyes; her story*

There was a strange contraction in her visceral region and then there was stillness. Deadly stillness. And no matter how many times I would pat her shoulders or caress her forehead she wouldn't open her eyes. She wouldn't open her eyes for one last time and see me love her...

It was incredibly cold that evening and I had a feeling I was waiting forever for him to come back home. When he did, his hands were busy, carefully handling something wrapped in a towel. He eventually made it into the room and then asked me to sit down. I already knew it was a gift and I had a feeling this would be special.

"You need to close your eyes love!"

"What is that?"

"Just do it!"

Patience wasn't one of my virtues although I had to spend an awful amount of my life curing my patients! But again that is past tense. At first it was a rounded up ball of fur and it was warm; a feeling very welcome in the freezing nights of January.

"Ou look! It has teeth"

"I bet she does. Took me a couple of bites and an hour to make her fall asleep in the car. Everything you would have imagined in our daughter, love!"

"..."

My husband wasn't the kind of person who had an awful lot of time for me but then he had this habit of surprising me with his deeds when I least expected them to. We had nothing to look forward to. Our only daughter, couldn't live to see the world outside her mother's protective womb. This little ball of fur, was more than welcome. She was the prettiest thing I ever saw in this world. I hugged on to her like she was the only thing I ever had in this world.

"Can you be a little careful love? She is just two weeks old and she just went through losing her mother. Her spine still needs a few days to be reinforced"

"Ou. I am so sorry little princess! That means she is like my daughter?"

"Technically no. But yes, her development needs lesser time than human beings. She will be an adult in 6 months' time and she wouldn't speak to human beings. And she might not yet just know the meaning of love. She is just a very good companion. Man's best friend as we know"

"No, she's my little princess. Full stop. And you shall treat her like one!"

Mornings were much busier trying to feed 'Alice'. Her mouth was awesomely small for spoons. I had to get a dropper from the shop. Milk was her favourite food and biscuits drenched in milk were just too delicious. My husband would keep watching I and Alice would do our morning ritual for almost an hour and then he would kiss my forehead and leave for his work. Alice, still a toddler would love to stay in my warm arms and wish 'papa' goodbye.

They say that even animals do their first call or in this case, a bark, when they know they are in a safe house, with their mother preferably. It took her almost a month to do so but it cleared our doubts about Alice. She could bark, and it has always been beautiful to listen to your child talk for the first time. It was like she was softly calling Maa. I remember Tatai doing it too, not barking but speaking. He called me 'Maa' for the first time when he was five and a half months old.

She grew up through all the vicissitudes of my life never leaving my side for a moment.

She was nibbling all over the house; preferably our ankles and the chair legs, the doors, the crockery, the iron chains, the shoes and all my favourite pens. But who cares! She was my daughter and I love her a lot. I let her exercise her teeth. When I scolded her she used to curl up herself and come to me. She knew I would be there for her when she needed me. She would curl down her otherwise straight ears and then dive into my lap while she was still young. But she always thought she was a kid even when she was larger than me; she would dive into my lap and look for solace in my arms. She loved me unconditionally.

Gradually she grew up to be a woman. She was a completely grown up adult and she grew up to be huge allegedly by onlookers. I still looked at her like a small ball of fur. Alice would wait for me to come and touch her food. That in turn would symbolize love towards her and then she would start eating. She would just not eat on her own and I would need to mother her all the time.

"Baby come to me. Alice baby. Where are you? Want to go to the terrace?"

And like a vibrant radiant skipper she would hop all the way to the roof. She was never tired when she was with me. She would jump up high to reach the leaves of the trees around and then keep biting the trophy she would acquire from her success attempts to jump.

She would keep chewing on the most valuable piece of equipment I had of my glorious career and I would just smile to her and say, "Alice!" and then the classy act of dropping one ear would happen. But I must admit the best part would be when I would take her in my arms and then hold her tight. She loved it as much as I did. I was going to sleep. My husband and I were already wrapped up in a blanket and Alice was busy doing something looking out of the window. The moment she noticed us together she jumped into the bed and inserted her nose between us; then her body and then just let herself fall on me. She was jealous. She just never wanted to share me with anyone, not even my husband. Tatai was treated like a sub-par breed. He was treated like an outsider. Alice knew I was hers only. I was lucky my husband loved her too and he would cuddle her up until Alice would look at me as if to say, "This man is not you Maa. Please love me. I need your arms while I go to sleep. Save me!"

Alice was too overprotective about me. My husband and my son were the only persons who could come near me. Others would experience the wrath of my daughter. She never bit anyone but even a harmless 'bark' from a member of her species, shepherd dogs used first in a region of North Eastern France, on the borders of Germany and Switzerland, called Alsace, would be enough to scare people to their death. German Shepherds or Alsatians are scary but cute fur balls.

Years passed by and I just forgot all the pain I had to endure in my life. I would smile and she would bark. I would shout and she would come to me, lick all over my face; make me feel loved. I would be blue and she would cuddle up my lap and sit there till I would be smiling. I would cry and she would cry with me whining like a lost puppy who has a sad mother. I would be happy and she would jump up in joy with me. I was no longer alone. I had my little princess always there with me.

Gradually as she grew up, she developed a rare case of paralysis in her lower limbs and when she was 10 years she lost the ability to use her lower limbs, completely. It is what we call hip dysplasia. I had to help her all the way along. She couldn't walk around with me but hell yes, she never let me alone. Eventually her voice (her bark as you the normal reader would refer to as) started showing signs of pain.

She went into complete coma after three months. Not a single voluntary muscle of hers moved. I was relieved to know she would be relieved of her pains soon. Although I couldn't stop my tears I never left her side. My husband was upstairs sleeping.

I took her in my arms and caressed her for the last time. She had a terrible muscle contraction and she vomited all over me. In the end when my tears were drowned under her agony there was silence. I looked into her eyes. She blinked her eyes twice as if to say something and then they closed. She would never look again or let me love her again.

Maybe she was waiting for me to take her into my arms before she would leave me forever, alone again. Maybe she just wanted to thank me for everything. Or maybe she just said, "I love you Mommy!"

Day 4

So what is life anyway?
What is faith? What is belief?

It's been four days that Maa has left us. Today I woke up with acceptance and calm. I looked at Baba and gave him a hug, patted Tua's head and then got up. The fact that Maa is not there is getting a bit easier to be accepted. The smell of incense sticks, the large gathering of people and the hue and cry over Maa's body is slowly being pushed into the distance; for good. I don't want to remember Maa as a heap of lifeless flesh and bones but as the woman who made my life a paradise.

So, what is life? Life is when one can feel, smell, see, touch, and taste. Life is when one can experience all emotions and make ones close to them feel emotions. Life is when one tries and protects themselves and protects their loved ones. Life is when one has memories associated with everything around them and when they interact with other 'alive' creatures, they make new memories. Life is when your vital organs are still functioning, at least that's how the world declares being alive to be. Life is when you can still think and your cognitive functions are still alive. Life is when you still want to go to a beautiful place and soak in the landscape.

Life is when you want to listen to a particular song and you ask your son, daughter, husband, wife or any other close people to find it for you. Life is when you remember how things were when you were young and how things have changed over time. Life is when you realise that you've outgrown many things and have suddenly turned into this old person, who isn't the young version you thought you were. Being alive is to yearn for some people and to be sad when they are not around you. Being alive is to passionately desire to want to eat something special, made by someone special, even if you know they are gone. Being alive is when you're vulnerable and open to wounds of the heart and soul. Being alive is when you can get up in the morning and silently cry, with tears streaming down your cheeks, while you assure yourself that the person closest to you is probably in a better place. Being alive is difficult.

Yesterday at Mamabari, they kept a little prayer for Maa and I was invited there. I didn't go during the prayer since Maa never loved these things. I went there long after these were done and I went to meet them. I laughed again, I enjoyed talking to them. It's been after fifteen to twenty years that so many of my favourite siblings are here at Mamabari. We spoke, we discussed and we laughed.

At the back of my head I feel guilty that I'm not grieving. I told this to Tulika and she just told me that she saw Maa in me yesterday. Maa never waited and wasted her life over grieving and I didn't as well. My smile resembled Maa's and I was moving on with life. Maa wouldn't want me to curl up in a ball and hide from the world while time passed me by... When Tuli said these, I was giving her a ride home. Immediately my eyes watered up but I realised she was right. It is but from the epitome of happiness that I learnt how to live. Grieving would've probably made her sad. She taught me that giving up on food or daily habits would not mean anything to someone dead, because they are gone. Paying respect to the dead happens internally.

A flashy funeral, 14 days of Hindu rituals or giving up on non-vegetarian food are just rules made up by stupid people at the top, long time back. She found no sense in them. Many people have questioned us for our decision not to hold any rituals and have absolutely frowned at us. In the end, I never believed in life after death and Maa never did. Maa wanted to go away in peace, when she would die, she told me. She wanted a peaceful meeting where people could come and speak, share their experiences with Maa. We organised that. That would be today.

I am not ready but I have to be. Maa will not mentally prep me anymore. Maa will not be there to look me in the eyes and then wipe my tears, hug me and send me right out to face the world. Behind all these layers of strength, lies a vulnerable child, who's learning to face the world. Maa suddenly tried to remove all those layers of adult pretence. Maa leaving us all, suddenly threw us into the fire! Life has to go on, I know, but I don't want to. I don't want to move on and I don't want to grieve. I'm confused what one should do. On the other hand, I'm sure that the 14 day ritual in Hindu tradition was designed to keep one busy after the death of their loved ones. They would be so busy the first 14 days that they would not be able to grieve. By the time they would find an empty space and empty room to grieve, the death of their loved ones would already be a distant memory that would take less effort to get over. I hate this. I would rather look at and touch everything that Maa and I shared, remember every bit of her and cry alone from the very first day, rather than pretending to satisfy her soul. We couldn't do anything to keep her alive, the system had already failed her. What's the point of appeasing a soul, when Maa was already gone.

Not that I would be able to hug her again, not that I would be able to sit behind her like when I was young, again. I wouldn't be able to eat cakes which she would bake again. I wouldn't be able to see birds and plants with her again. I would never go to the mountains with her, again. I would never see the sea again, with Maa. I would never hug her again. She will never kiss me again and I'll never be with her again!

Even on the day of her death, she was almost about to do another miracle. It couldn't be completed, once again due to the red-tapism and extreme carelessness in the medical profession. Maa had beautiful kind eyes. She was a better spotter than most wildlife guides. She could spot a tiger in a forest, before alarm calls would begin and before the guides would even think about it.

Catharsis with Maa

She wanted to donate her eyes. Baba had informed them way before, right after Maa left us. They couldn't get their support team to come over, even after 6 hours and as we know, after 6 hours the cornea dies. Maa's last wish remained unfulfilled but it's not a bad one. I could see her with her eyes on. Eyes reminded me of something else though. I wish, through some strange device I could be transported into the world of Naruto. Maa leaving us, is the biggest single incident that put me into a state of permanent shock. It could have triggered my 'mangekyo sharingan'[39] and probably a 'rinnegan'[40] after that. I could have probably used 'rinne rebirth'[41] after that! Who knows...

Maa's perpetual smile haunts me. Her ability to smile, even when terribly hurt or ill was what made her look invincible. It also made us unable to understand what she

---

[39] Mangekyo Sharingan – a special visual prowess exclusive to the Uchiha clan in the anime series Naruto by Masashi Kishimoto

[40] Rinnegan - a special visual prowess exclusive to the Uchiha clan in the anime series Naruto by Masashi Kishimoto; the user of it can even control eternal life

[41] Rinne Rebirth – a special visual prowess exclusive to the Uchiha clan in the anime series Naruto by Masashi Kishimoto, one of the features of the rinnegan; the user can bring back the dead.

was going through. We never understood she was in pain, in retrospect.

When Baba looks at her last few pics now, he says that it looks like Maa's face looks swollen. I just told him it was the width of the lens that creates distortion.

While I know his camera is not one to shine such distortions, I had to lie to protect him from himself.

Maa looked tired though and she looked like she could use a hug. Not sure why doctors think they are invisible but they should also start caring for themselves.

This is unbearable. Maa was careless with herself, not others! Simple follies, lead to such huge losses.

I teach linguistics. I teach the intricate balance between life and communication. I try to understand the intermingling of language and society. Like cars, trucks and flights and rockets run on petroleum, hydrogen or electricity, we run on ATP[42].

It is the currency by which we operate. Life operates on a different currency. Its currency is what we call language. Right from communication; to preservation, memory and thinking... everything is carried out using language.

---

[42] ATP – adenosine triphosphate. Let me break it down for you. Mitochrondia in our cells produce ATP in order for us to survive. It is simply put, energy.

When a person dies, all parts of their parole, as a part of the bigger Saussurian[43] langue[44], dies with them. That parole will never be breached again or used. Language enables one to be able to communicate, think, preserve, protect and be oneself. The emblazoning of character, the building of one's social identity and the characterisation of the world, begins using language; ends with language. It's what runs the mortal realm. It's the symbolic currency that entitles us to everything we have ever done in life.

---

[43] Ferdinand de Saussure – the founder of structuralism. He propounded that language is a system of signs where a signifier (a recalling system) is associated with a signified (a core concept) over time. He speaks about other core concepts like the langue and the parole, the syntagmatic and paradigmatic and so on. There can also be sign relation kinds like icons, indexes and symbols, according to Charles Saunders Pierce, a structuralist who came later. Read "A course in General Linguistics" by Saussure (published posthumously in 1916) for further details.

[44] Langue – an imaginary repertoire containing all languages, all traditions, all cultures, all probable utterances, thoughts in the entirety of time and all sorts of knowledge that ever existed in the entirety of time. This is a concept by Saussure.

Day 5

The day hundreds cried at her memorial

It's been five days since Maa has left us. I haven't cried today, at least not yet. Thousands of people spoke yesterday to share their memories with Maa. I keep fixating. I keep repeating how awesome she was and how much of a guide she was to me. Yesterday I realised how much of a guide and social support she was to thousands of people. Many people broke down on the stage, at the dais. Many people smiled while sharing experiences with Maa. I was left amazed at her fan following and at the way she was loved by everyone. Suddenly it doesn't seem like a pain I have to bear alone anymore. Unfortunately, it will be a pain I'll have to bear alone. She was closest to me and that, nothing will change. Masimoni and Chotomama broke down at the dais. I spoke! I spoke on how the Sapir and Whorf hypothesis sensibly destroys and deconstructs the whole world. I spoke how the intermingling of early society taught us to grieve and how the insinuations of the first human beings gave us a bearing into death, through language.

When I woke up today but my eyes didn't open yet, I suddenly heard Maa speak. I probably just was leaving rem sleep and slowly becoming conscious. My brain played tricks with me. I eventually woke up to, of course, see Maa not there. I tried to close my eyes again, so as to see Maa again. My body, my soul, my everything yearns for Maa, wants her to come back in her corporal form again... At the memorial organised for her yesterday, I remembered something sweet. When I was young, many a times Maa had performed there. She had such amazing pronunciation and control over pitch variations. She was amazing at reciting Tagore and other Bengali poets. Her voice brought many solace! Eventually I was taken back to those old days when I would sit beside Maa and ask her, " Kokhon shesh hobe Maa?" (When will this be over Maa); and how can I forget the food packets she would get. Everywhere Maa was a participant, i.e., she recited, she would get food packets and I would be the primary contender for those. When Tua was born, that was shared and I was happy about it, but right now, there is a huge hole we both cannot fill up. No one will take us to amazing gatherings, bring food packets with amazing food for us, or not enjoy themselves because their son and daughter are not! How can one woman be this selfless? I mean, what the hell?!

I wanted to sing yesterday but I couldn't. I knew I would break down. "Tumi robe nirobe"[45], Tagore's rendition of how a person doesn't die and how they stay with us in spite of us being vocal about it or not, is a song Maa loved. I didn't hear the song play around me in the last 5 days but

---

[45] A beautiful song by Tagore, now available on Youtube, sung by multiple singers in a plethora of styles.

I'm sure if that plays, I'll break down and I'll go through a cathartic exposition. I'll go through whatever though. I wish I could go through everything and get Maa back. I wish such platonic expositions could give rise to life and that such risings could bring back the dead. I guess my ramblings have some sort of anti-climactic effect on my expectations though. It's been five days since Maa is gone but I guess my bearings are taking shape. I'm starting to realise, Maa won't come back again. When I close my eyes, I can still see Maa but my expectations of being in her arms, is slowly depreciating.

Baba lied to me. When I was done with the security check at the Delhi airport, I kept on calling everyone to know how Maa was doing. I wanted to know what was the current prognosis and what the doctors were doing to stabilize her. I smelled a rat when I suddenly found that everyone's phone was switched off. There were tears in my eyes, expecting the worst but I held on to my wits, grit my teeth and waited. The boarding gate opened and it I walked into the flight. Mine was the last seat and I sat down.

I called Kaku. He didn't pick up the phone. Baba did. Baba asked me if I was seated and within seconds, immediately broke down and told me he was afraid to lose Maa. He was afraid they wouldn't be able to save Maa. I told I was on the way and asked him to be strong. The phone was disconnected. I didn't know Maa was already dead by then, but, at that point in time, tears came down my face and I screamed inside my head. I was shattered. Even if Baba lied, I knew what the truth was, at the back of my head. It's absurd how a person you've just spent 31 years of your life with, born out of is suddenly just a mass of nerves, muscles and bones. It's absurd how a lifeless body lies, in front of you and memories keep gushing into your mind as you do. It's absurd how the human mind works.

Day 6

It's a new world out there

Six days have passed by since Maa left us for a better home, in the form of primal elements, at corners of the earth, flowing with the wind, mixing with water, breathing in space like a candle in the wind. I haven't had so many incidents where I broke down. As days are passing by, it's getting less difficult to control oneself, but, unfortunately it's getting easier to pretend smile. The permanent stricture stuck on my face is quintessentially emotionless. Waking up and finding out every day that Maa is not here and speaking to oneself to calm oneself down is getting less difficult.

I didn't want to attend another memorial held for Maa yesterday. I wanted to stay home, stay alone and just be with myself. I didn't want to pretend like I was strong all evening and sit down and smile, while others shared experiences with Maa. I wanted some peace. Everybody wanted to go and hence I obliged. They organised a special program for Maa on world dramatics day. They sang songs, they read our poetry and in the end, there was a thirty mins presentation playing some dramatic involvements by Maa. I was instantly reminded of some memories. Long back when Maa used to go to Nandan[46] or Rabindra Sadan[47] for her programs, she used to take me along. "Why is it called a green room Maa?", I asked as I was told it was the green room where we waited. I was expecting to enter a green coloured room but to my disappointment, it was a rather normal room without any sort of green colour. Maa said it was a waiting room for artists. I didn't realise it till now, how big of an artist Maa was. I am nowhere close to her. I used to stand at the backstage, while Maa would perform her poetry, poetry that every person would praise and have tears in eyes, listening to. Maa brought stories alive. Maa brought life into poetry. Her way of reciting brought such an eerie uncanny breath of freshness to otherwise 'normal' poetry. Less people understand poetry. Maa understood the actual nature of poetry.

Maa looked at me and in disappointment told me that her new phone was a disaster. It didn't work as expected and that it should be sent back. I looked into her issues. I always did. I was her one stop tech prob solver and her everything solver. I didn't come across any issues. Eventually I realised the problem she was facing was with adjusting to the new system. She was eventually adjusting to the new phone, a new operating system and she wasn't ready to adjust. Typically Maa!! There were no issues

---

[46] A famous venue for stage performances in Kolkata

[47] Another famous venue for stage performances in Kolkata, named after the Nobel laureate Rabindranath Tagore

with the phone. She wasn't ready to come out of the soft cocoon of familiarity. For the past six days, I've been reminded multiple times that Maa is no more and that life will be much more difficult without her. I wasn't ready to leave the familiarity too. I guess it runs in the blood. But just like Maa was forced to exit her cocoon of familiarity and explore the new world, I and Baba have been forcefully ejected from the system of parental and marital care; respectively. It's a new world out there.

Coping Mechanisms

Everybody has their own

I had a fight with Baba yesterday. He's been coping in a very different way. From the day Maa left us, he's been trying to fill up her shoes. Not that he cannot, but he's been unendingly trying to make sense. He's been trying to get things back to normal. He's been trying to get some semblance out of the whole equation called life. Maa's absence has absolutely absorbed him. It's not that it hasn't, us, but if it's a race, Baba has lost many more memories than us. Baba has been forcing me and Tuli to get things forwarded regarding our wedding. He wants us to work right now to get the cards printed, get the menu fixed, talk to the organisers and finalize everything. I was at first very pissed with him for having no respect for Maa and that it's only been a couple of days. When I shouted at him, he left the room and slept in peace for some time. But soon, I realised my mistake and that Baba was just trying to fill in his unfathomable voids. He was just trying to make sure the absence of activities would not make him enter a state of delirium and a state of remembrance. He just wanted life to go on as usual. Just like how Google maps allows you to recentre a map and come back to the track you were using, Baba is desperately looking for a recentre button for his life. We have moved so far away from the actual track that we are all looking for a recentre button. There's a bug in the system. There's no recentre. No one will fix that. This journey will go on, with the new bearings. Life will have to navigate a new route for itself.

Multiple authors, over time have delved into the idea of death. Maa's leaving us has forced me to contemplate and dive into the idea of death myself. What is death? What makes you think one is dead? Well, I think the absence of life is death. The absence of everything that makes you feel alive is death. The absence of joyfulness, the absence of happiness, the inability of making new memories with Maa, the absence of a lot many more things and the absence of Maa is death; death in a much more metaphorical form. But with death comes the concept of new life. I still reiterate that I do not believe in the concept of eternal life, life after death or resurrection but I do believe that with one life being spent, another is already forming using the same elements. This has to do with law of conservation of energy, not with life after death. Rearranging the atoms of Maa through some chemical process and turning her into the elements set her free from her corporal body but somewhere someone is still waiting for a baby, a baby which is slowly through biochemistry going through cell regeneration and multiplication. The baby is growing up. And just like the vanquishing of elements, this baby is growing up by using the elements. Every death, every birth is just the law of conservation of energy being observed in real life.

Catharsis with Maa

I'm afraid that if I don't write down any part of this, what I'm writing, I'll lose a part of Maa. I don't want to. I've been writing, writing and writing, rambling, rambling and rambling ever since she died. It's very difficult to still grasp that she's no more here with me, while I'm writing this, suddenly asking me what I'm doing with my phone, all day. She's not here reading her magazines or a random book of poetry. She's not here scrolling up her limitless feed of birds, plants and food. She's not here to suddenly ask me to get up and take a bath. She's not here to run her fingers through my hair, ask me to get a haircut, trim my beard, take her somewhere amazing, discuss our wedding with me or to just talk about ridiculously disgusting things with me. She's just not here. I cry every time I am told or made to understand she's not here but I know that no amount of crying will bring her back to me. Nothing will give me solace. There's so less!

I look everywhere to just find, borderlines hallucinations happening to me. I keep on imagining Maa everywhere, just the way she used to sit in her red with yellow striped house coat. I imagine her screaming at Tua for being late and lackadaisical at everything and I sometimes almost hear her talking to me. I imagine her telling me how fed up she's with Baba's smoking habit. I imagine her reading out poetry at times. I imagine her watering her plants. I imagine her gently rubbing the leaves of plants to clean them of dust and mealybugs. I imagine her holding me and crying, when she would be sad. Sometimes I just talk to her and respond her answers to myself. My eyes tear up when I respond for her and i know it's stupid but it is that it is. When I was driving everyone to the memorial organised for Maa yesterday, everyone was there in the car but Maa. I looked at the seat beside the driver's and Maa wasn't there. The car still has a doctor's logo and everything she used to take to get clinic, hospital and chambers. That car also saw so much of Maa. There's no place I can go that's devoid of her memories. It's difficult to imagine that the Maa in the form of her body, made so many beautiful memories in my life and suddenly that corporal form doesn't exist anymore. It's hard to imagine that the woman I used to hug while I was sad and hold close does not exist in this world. I mean, I can do everything and I can travel to the darkest and farthest corners of Earth but there will be nowhere that would hide Maa. Maa is just gone. She's stopped existing and she's stopped being in existence.

Day 7

One week since incident

It's been a week since Maa has left us. It doesn't seem like a distant memory but in time, eventually, it will seem like a part of life, which was done with, which happened because it had to and which was unfortunate. A year later, I would probably be smiling on the day Maa died, unlike today. A decade later, I along with Tuli, might be playing with our kid. Tuli might behave just like Maa with our kid, since they both shared so many traits of character. Strong women think and behave alike. Hundred years later, no one will know about this minor death which inconvenienced so many people, which broke so many people. Today our home kitchen is functioning as usual. There's the sound of fish being fried in hot oil and of lentils being boiled on the gas. Life went on, as usual, though on a new uncentred route. That morning I didn't have milk but today I had milk as usual. Maa isn't here to talk to me though. She never will be.

This morning I woke up to the voice of Maa. No, it wasn't a recording or someone listening to her recite. It was her, calling out to me, directly! I believe it was a hallucination or I was dreaming. I was in rem sleep then. I suddenly heard Maa asking me to wake up since it was already 8am.

I woke up to realise Maa, as the person turned into a signified, untouchable furthermore by human hands. I realised she was gone. I froze! I looked to find that Baba was still sleeping. I went to him with watery eyes and peacefully adored his forehead for some time. I realised this is more difficult than I can imagine it to be. Just like a house seems perfectly fine when termites infest it's foundations, making it hollow from the inside, Maa's death made me hollow from the inside, while I keep pretending everything is absolutely fine. She completed me and now, her absence is eating me from the inside. I washed a few of my cloths yesterday. In the past, when Maa was alive, she used to tell me to leave them be and she would wash them when she would wash hers. I told to myself that, that would never happen again. It's now my responsibility to wash them, along with Baba's. Maa won't help us anymore. Rather, Maa won't be able to help us anymore. We have to bank on self-sufficiency. The faster we learn how to cope with circumstances without Maa, the better off we will be sooner.

I regret shifting to Gurgaon in the recent past. I should have spent a lot more time with Maa. She was not sad that I had left for a better opportunity but she just knew she would miss me. I remember the day we left for Gurgaon in my car from home. She was standing, looking at me while I sat in the driver's seat. I hugged her and kissed her forehead and told her, "Maa I will see you soon." I regret taking up this offer to teach since this stole me from Maa. She needed me so much and I left her alone with her plants. Probably Baba being away at Cooch Behar and I being at Gurgaon forced Maa to befriend these beautiful plants. Maa probably hated being alone in her old age. She turned 60 just months back. She didn't retire from her job but she retired from life too soon. It wasn't her time. I regret not having spent more time with Maa. I will have to regret making a few decisions. I'll have to live with them.

My table is filled with things right now, the table in my room at Chinsurah and I don't want to clean it anymore. It's filled with things from Maa and I'd hate for those to be thrown away since they have been touched by Maa. I've never been this sentimental. I've always thrown away things which are not of use. At best, I've given things away which are not useful to me, but I've never kept things. Right now I've kept Maa's cloths, the ones she wore, inside a polythene packet. I've saved dad's handkerchief he used to clean Maa's face when she was already gone. I have saved so many things. Every morning I open that polythene, just to smell it and feel Maa once again. One day the smell will vanish. Little bacteria will probably have destroyed the atoms of smell or probably they will just erode away. Her memories will remain, nothing else will.

One morning I was out with Maa, like many other mornings with Maa. She asked me to stop the scooty at a particular place in Chandannagore, specifically near Khalisani. There's this beautiful bamboo grove there. We parked the two wheeler and ventured into the bamboo grove. She was so happy. And like always, she kept collecting plants from there too. I rebuked her reminding her that there were too many plants already and she need not collect more, to which she responded sharply saying,"Gach thakle praan thaake tatai. Gach konodin beshi hobe na" (If there are plants, there is life Tatai. There will never be enough plants). I never helped her with potting a plant, like ever. I would sit there while she would pot plants, try and save the ones which are dying with ample support. I could feel her pain when she would show me a plant and tell me that it died. I could feel her exclaimant glee when she would show me beautiful plants and be happy throughout the evening. I could feel her loneliness when I was at Gurgaon and Baba was at his work place. I could feel how much she missed me and Baba, when we were away. I cannot feel her anymore! She's not there.

I'm leaving on Friday, by Howrah Rajdhani, back to my place of work. I remember when I used to return, Maa used to accompany me to Howrah station. I would hate for her and Baba to come and see me off but I just couldn't hate her coming with me. I knew I wouldn't see her for the next few months or so, and those last few hours with her would be something I would love and hence I never asked her not to come. Sometimes I would hold her and cry. I remember running back to her to hug her multiple times when the train would leave. I would hug Baba too. And I remember how it felt like hugging her for a couple of seconds and realising that they were not enough. There was this once when the local train stopped one kilometre away from Howrah and it was almost time for my scheduled train to leave from Howrah (we live in a suburb and we have to go to Howrah to avail express trains). I hugged Maa and I jumped into the track, ran with all my belongings. When I reached the station, the train was already in motion and my throat was extremely dry. I threw my bag into one of the open doors and I jumped into another. I called Maa and told her I was fine. She sounded relieved. I realised her train would still be stranded there. I came to the door of the train and I saw her, still standing there at the door. Somehow she knew I would come out to see her. As the trains passed by, I called Maa and she just asked me to take care. I will never be able to call Maa to ask her to take care and she will never be able to ask me to stay well and take care. Those things are in the past now.

Maa loved visiting JNU[48]. All the while when I was a student, Maa loved staying inside JNU. She loved the flowers there, the beautiful campus, the sticky oily smell from Periyar and Bramhaputra, the momos from 24x7, the tea from Ganga dhaba and the shawarma from north east. She loved it all.

---

[48] The author completed his Masters, MPhil and Phd from Jawaharlal Nehru University (JNU) and hence his family visited the university often. Ganga Dhaba is a famous eatery there. Periyar is a gent's hostel at JNU. Bramhaputra is a gent's PhD scholar hostel at JNU. 24x7 is an eatery at JNU (once upon a time it was open 24x7 but new administration severely mannered it back to 'normal' timings. North East is another eatery from JNU, one where the author used to go to eat Shawarmas and Alungsas.

Day 8

She didn't know

It's been eight days. It's time that I go through the memory lane. I'm leaving on Friday and time is running short. Time running away has always been the one thing constant in our lives. Looking at the person you loved the most, lying down lifeless is painful.

Experiencing the death of the person you loved the most is excruciating and you feel like you're dead too, but what is even more heart-breaking is to have to sort through the things they used. Everything you pick up have a memory attached to them. I picked up her sweaters and smelled them, in expectation that they would not be washed but unfortunately they were cleaned and packed. Maa didn't know she will never return. She stacked her bed, full of cloths; full of cloths to be packed and stacked into the attic. She never did that. This morning I gathered the courage to enter her room and finally sort out everything. I wore a few of her cloths and when I fit in a few of them, I wore them. I suddenly decided to wear a few of them and kept them aside. One particular overcoat was large and I fit in it. I put my hands in its pocket, just like anyone would do to check out the fit and in that pocket was a lipstick, a handkerchief and an N95 face mask.

My eyes watered up the moment I realised she was not ready to die. She knew she would return home to us, the people she called her family. She would come home, share her stories and she would wait for everyone to hear them. She would call me and share beautiful stories of the journey or how Baba didn't click a picture of a bird, she had spotted. She would tell me how my sister is still lazy and never completed any task on time. She would keep rambling about how her sister, 'Masimoni' is always late and always complaining about things. She would tell me that the driver drove so bad and she felt like she would puke. She would say, she should have come to Delhi to meet me instead. But she never said anything.

Packing her things into neat packets and sticking them up with a cello tape was just like packing her memories up and sending them down to repression town. I constantly had tears in my eyes while I was packing Maa's stuff. I had this eerie fear in me that I was destroying her memories and if those went into the attic, they will never come out again. Maa would be forgotten.

I kept revisiting memory lane and reliving how Maa asked either me or Baba for help for getting our winter cloths out of the attic. In our absence she got them out herself and I always complained to her how dangerous it was for her to climb on the shaky ladder we had. This is a fear I do not have to live with anymore.

The bed is now clean; clean from the last mess she ever made. Maa thought she would clean it when she would return. She never did. I did it, like always. But like other times, she never helped me hand over the plastic bags while I climbed up the ladder. Tua helped. Maa could not.

◆

Day 9

Trying to smile while my world just died!

It's been nine days today. For the last couple of months, I was very concerned about Maa. I was concerned that she would fall off her scooty and get hurt. She already got disbalanced twice or thrice and developed sprains in her ankle. I was pissed but I knew riding her scooty was the easy option for her and the large car wouldn't fit in, everywhere.

I always had this at the back of my head that someday, suddenly I'll get the news of some accident and Maa would be home with a broken hand or leg. Now I wish, she broke a hand or leg and came back home. Bloody murderers, they murdered my Maa with incorrect diagnosis and treatment.

Bloody murderers! Bloody wolves in sheep's clothing. Bloody corporate goons. Had it not been for their oversight, Maa would still be here.

Maa would probably be whatsapping me random pictures of flowers or birds and would tell me how she had a novel experience somewhere. She would also tell me to be happy and safe.

Catharsis with Maa

When I would come back home, I preferred sleeping at night with both Maa and Baba. I used to turn my back towards Maa. I would let Maa hold me from behind, curl up into the natal position and pretend like Maa is still encompassing me in her womb. She would hold me tight while still half asleep and keep holding me and go off to full sleep. I would be able to feel her breath on my nape and somehow

I would know I'm where I want to be. I would feel safe, protected and loved. Last night, when I suddenly woke up, Tua looked like Maa. In the darkness, all colours are muted and all colours look like shades of blue and dark grey with localised umbra regions. My mind played tricks on me. I felt like it was Maa. But I knew, it wasn't her. How I yearned to suddenly feel her warmth! How I yearned for her love!

The transfer of knowledge and information through language is something that is a result of displacement in language. Charles Hockett[49] would have been proud of me now. Humans are capable of spreading information in a designated time and space and also beyond.

---

[49] Charles Hockett - The propounded of design features in language. These are universal features of language which define the very nature of languages, starting from the most basic of functions that a language must imbibe to features of language that correlate to lying (prevarication) and the most important of them all which is displacement.

We are allegedly the only species that protects and saves information in books and in clouds. We are the only species that prevaricates[50]. We are the only species with rituals, theories, axioms and enlightenment. An individual is capable of interpretations using the already existing body of vast knowledge. I'm probably referring to the rational system of knowledge interpretation in human beings.

Maa will never displace her story to me again. Maa will remain a history and live on through us. Her mind will no longer transmit information. The information she never spread died with her.

Her secrets died with her. Had she been the last speaker of a language, the language would have died with her. And she was! She was the last speaker of a language for me, that needs a mother to exist. I'll forever wander the mortal realm without Maa now, devoid of stories, love, recitations, hugs and songs.

Maa and Alice were very close. Alice was two months old when she was brought to our home. Her mother died as a result of birthing eight pups. Six died and two survived.

---

[50] Prevaricate – to lie. One of the major design features of language by Charles Hockett. Hockett propounds that this is the feature that allows human beings to use displacement, another feature in his long list, to lie about things. It must be noted that human beings are the only species capable of lying. Other species can technically play 'possum' but not lie about things that are removed from them in space and in time.

Alice was one of the two. From the very first day we fell in love with her innocence and her frivolous attitude.

She was the daughter Maa never had and Maa loved her like her own. I loved her like my sibling and Maa even made food for us in the same bowl. We, of course, didn't eat from the same bowl, but frankly, I wouldn't mind. Alice died in 2011. Maa was right there with Alice when she died. Probably now, in another dimension they are together. Probably, in a life after death Maa is with her long lost daughter, playing with Alice and holding her tight in her arms. I wish I could believe that. I wish I could find solace in these thoughts, but, unfortunately, life is ephemeral and I might probably die by the time I accept ontological realities instead of the epistemological realities. Maa raised me as an empirically fuelled rational individual who would literally question everything, till they would be satisfied. She taught me to be irritating, in short. I blame Maa! Had she raised me like other kids, I'd be happy believing that Maa is alive in another life, with Alice, my long lost furry sister.

I remember, when I was young, Maa was posted at Bansberia and on the days without school I would eagerly sit down while Maa draped herself in sarees. I would literally act like an irritating kid and ask her all sort of questions regarding sarees but what I would wait for would be to help her wrap her saree around her waist. That, for me, being allowed to help her was no less than being given the nuclear codes in order to start the third world war, or being given the highest authority in a geographical area to unanimously keep changing names of places! Maa knew how much I loved doing that. She would let me! When I grew up, I didn't do that anymore but I used to be Maa's personal driver. I used to get a lot of practise in driving and Maa used to get a driver.

I loved helping that woman, in whatever ways possible. She was sort of unhinged. It was ridiculously difficult helping a woman who was superbly self-sufficient. She taught me the definition of being self-sufficient. She taught me to love oneself and taught me that while staying like an island isn't what human beings are made for, we are also needed to pretend to be okay at times, with a smile on our face while the world is silently fading away at times. I'm probably practising exactly that right now; trying to smile while my world just died!

Day 10

I remember how she spoke, how she laughed...

It's been ten days since Maa went through a massive cardiac arrest and her heart beat for the last time and even today I still open my eyes imagining Maa is right beside me. Even today, my mind knows that she's gone but my body hasn't gotten over the procedural memory of being with Maa, in her love for the last thirty one years. How can one forget the woman they loved the most, so soon? But alas, soon you forget the way they spoke and the way they laughed. Soon you forget the way they walked. A couple of days more and you forget the way they shouted at you when they wanted you to be better. Couple of days yet more and you start accepting that life has to go one without them. In the end what you're left with are fond memories and regret that their beautiful life was cut short. I, on the other hand haven't even forgotten the way she used to talk.

I remember how she spoke, how she laughed, how she ate, how she sang, how she recited poetry, how she scolded me, how she mocked, how she mimicked various animals and confused them, how she hugged me and how she was cold, lifeless and dead the last time, I kissed her checks and forehead goodbye and saw her for the last time before her body would be forwarded into the furnace. I guess, a part of me is still there waiting for Maa to walk out and hug me, tell me things are okay and this was all a dream; while another part of me is desperately trying the get over Maa's untimely death.

I hopelessly look at Maa's pictures. It feels like she's on a trip, somewhere She is still smiling, waiting to return home to me and to everyone. And then there's this subtle yet strong reminder of how I saw her body disappear for the last time. I remember her body burning to a crisp. She is gone.

I yearn to hear her voice now. Listening to her recordings do no justice to the beautiful voice she had and how she used to call me, "Dushtu chele" (naughty boy) when I was young. I miss her. I miss every bit of her. I'm not sure when I can stop missing her. I don't think I will ever be ready to stop missing her. I was never ready to lose her. Baba didn't switch off Maa's phone. While it would be excruciatingly difficult for me to gather the courage to call Maa's phone, Baba wants me to do that. He says the only difference will be that he will pick up the call. Maa won't. For me that's a world of difference. How can I tell Baba that my world has stopped existing! How can I tell Maa that I miss her? How can I tell her that I need her to be there in my wedding? Who will fill in her shoes? Who will cry in happiness and hug us when I just get married to Tulika? Who will solve all her gynaecological issues? Who will hold both of us when we return home? Who will bring incense sticks to the main gate when I bring Tulika home? Where is she?

Catharsis with Maa

Whenever Baba is narrating the story of how Maa was treated at the hospital, I can't but feel guilty about how Maa was counting her days, unknowingly. She was helpless. Maa wanted to be shifted to Kolkata, where her friends are. She wanted her friends to treat her, supposedly back to normalcy. She didn't want to die. She didn't know she has exactly a few days to live when she was admitted to the hospital in Siliguri. Eventually when Baba progresses with the date from the day of Maa's first admission which was on the 16 of March to the day she died on 22 of March, I feel like someone is pulling my guts out. Listening to Baba narrate the story of how Maa died is absolutely heart rending. She was conscious till 4.40 am and then her mind slowly absolved into oblivion. She eventually lost her mind and dived deep into an unfathomable abyss.

For once I wish I believed life after death. Yeah. What more can I do. Her absence is killing me. I've done so many things with her that now doing them alone is so difficult. I've stopped myself from texting her so many times; texting her how much I miss her and texting her how broken I am but in the end the text would reach Baba and it would only break him even more. I did not want to break him even more. I went up to the terrace and called her out twice today. I had forgotten she was there. I had forgotten her body didn't exist anymore. I had forgotten she had died.

I'm sure Maa never read Chaucer's Canterbury Tales[51] or the story of Chanticleer but there's this bird and its call sounds just like it's saying Chanticleer. I will probably get to know eventually what bird it was that Maa referred to as Chanticleer[52] but it will not be from Maa. Sometimes I lose my mind.

Alice was so protective about Maa that she would literally not let anyone touch Maa. I kind of hated that since I wanted Maa too and we fought a lot, literally. I used to beat her up and she used to scare me. She never bit me though! Maa made me realise that animals are to be loved. There was this once when Maa told me something. It's something I'll never forget. "Animals can't talk, can't share, can't express. You can. Beating up her is inhuman and means you haven't become a human". That day I cried a lot. Maa cried because Alice was hurt. I never beat up Alice again or any other animal. Everyone knows I'm always talking to dogs and that dogs are attracted to me but they don't know what started it all. It was Maa. After Alice died, Baba wanted to get another dog for Maa but she didn't want another. She told Baba that bringing another dog would never replace her daughter. Everywhere she went, she was flocked by dogs. We rightly said that Alice was in Wonderland. Maa treated her like she would treat me and the only difference is that

---

[51] Geofrrey Chaucer – considered by many to be the first sociolinguist. He by himself is an epoch in English literature!

[52] Chanticleer – a character from the Canterbury Tales.

she wasn't human. Maa's care for her was beyond what a mother would do for a human child.

When I was young, Baba was still doing some research and we were far from affluent. Maa and Baba used to occasionally take me to Kolkata by local train. I would, like a petulant child walk to the window and wait for Maa to substantiate my decision to stop everyone else staring out of the window by walking to the window and standing in front of it, as if it was mine. Maa, had to support me while I used to embarrass her by doing what I did. Today when Baba and Tua came to see me off at the station, I remembered everything and Maa wasn't there. On such occasions, Maa used to be sad. She would be sad that her son would be leaving. Today when I am sitting by the train window alone, without blocking anyone else's view, without embarrassing Maa, she isn't there to even talk, over phone. No one is calling me and bothering me about how I'm seated or if my luggage is safe. Maa isn't there to ask me. Today I'm seated by the window, but I have no one to share that beautiful experience with. Today when the rail tracks look like they are dancing, Maa isn't here to explain to me what's happening. Today when I'm travelling, I'm truly travelling alone. Look Maa, I grew up! Won't you see?

I used to love train journeys when I was young. I loved everything related to trains. Now, there are so many memories with Maa in train, that it's impossible to travel and keep myself from thinking about her. Once I boarded the train, I suddenly found people talking to their loved ones. Now is ideally when I would have called Maa. Now is ideally when I would call her and explain that things are fine and I am seated perfectly. I would explain how I'm still wearing a mask and I would eventually ask her to take care of herself. I wish I could. The person opposite to me, is holding a long conversation with their mother and it kills me inside to not be able to talk to Maa. Discussing everyday chores, discussing life, discussing people, discussing the neighbourhood aunty, discussing her work and discussing everything under the sky is something I want right now but Maa won't ever talk again. I'll have to live the rest of my life knowing that I'll never talk to my Maa again. I'll have to accept that Maa is gone.

The setting sun was once upon a time symbolised with the victory of darkness over light. The whole system of paganism was primarily based on nature and the fight between light and dark kept creeping into ontological mythology. Every morning the Sun god wins over the darkness and every evening the darkness wins over the sun. The cycle of this eternal fight has been going on for centuries. Someday that will end too. Time is a cruel protagonist and we are all little pawns in time's massive dial of events. Today when I'm looking at the Sun, it reminds me of Maa. She was my Sun. She made my life bright and she made my life worthwhile. Losing her has cast me into darkness, but just like the eternal cycle of light and dark, this too shall pass. Someday I'll once again be in her arms. I don't have to miss her and more. I won't miss her any more.

Day 11

Much loved characters are seldom real

It's been eleven days and I woke up to the sound of a metallic ring. I'm in train, en-route Delhi. Me returning is more like trying to fix an amputated hand with a couple of band aids but it has to do for now. Maa would wake up early in the morning, even in trains and she would keep looking outside the large windows. She would keep spotting birds, animals, strange places, beautiful trees and a lot of other things. Had I known that my time with her is limited, I would definitely wake up earlier and spend time with her. On some journeys, I woke up and lied down in her lap while she did her shenanigans but in some I didn't. She was never alone in her journeys except for her final journey. I wish we could accompany her. I just hope she didn't die alone, in that room thinking no one tried to do anything to save her. Baba told me how she was gasping for her breath and how everyone tried to save her and how the oversight on the part of a corporate doctor allowed Baba and Kaku to try and transport Maa, a patient with acute renal and liver failure, through road transport in a journey over 14 hours. Terrible oversight! Maa was in pain and when I spoke to her hours before she was gone, she explained that her left hand was paining. Later on many of Maa's doctor colleagues explained that it might be due to an ischemic heart condition that the left hand was paining terribly. Baba and Kaku didn't know. They aren't doctors. But this is a classic case of ischemic heart condition. During her journey from Siliguri to Ranaghat, she kept complaining about how the doctors never spoke to Maa, consulted her, even if she's been a practising government doctor for more than twenty five years. Her experience was watered down the drain. She was murdered by a couple of inexperienced killers who call themselves doctors, the same way Maa did. I don't agree. It's too late to try anything now. The damage has been dealt. A severe damage has been dealt to all of us.

"Mathay ekta tang korey marbo" (I will hit your head and it will ring like a bell), Maa told Tua. Tua was sitting at the dining table and her finger slowly crept into her nose, without her realising because it was her habit. I saw her doing it too but Tua didn't realise she did it. Maa looked at her and made a scary face. "Mummum I didn't do it. I just itched the outside of my nose", tua explained. Maa hated lies and explaining or covering lies. That's when Maa said that. It was so funny that I almost fell out of my chair.

This, when I deboard the train would be when Maa would call me. She would call me and ask me if I'm on time, if the train journey was tiring, she would share a bit of her experience and she would go on narrating what she did in the morning. Today, everyone else called me but Maa didn't. She never will. Sitting in the Delhi airport metro express line brings back memories of how excited Maa was to be in this train, the first time; excited because there

Catharsis with Maa

were a lot of birds on the electric lines that day; excited because she could see monuments and roads and people. She loved life. She loved to live her life, one day at a time, like it was her last. In the end, she lived so many last days that her last day in her body was a day she could not live to the fullest. Such a waste of life energy. Her way of life inspired me to always smile, always be happy and always forget the bad parts. She taught me to be a better man. In a world of patriarchs, she was the feminist force who taught me gender roles first and then systematically deconstructed their roles to bring out actual gender equality.

She taught me to live, to love, to eat, to do literally everything in life. It's strange how I'm desperately looking for a remnant of Maa, like she exactly was gasping for air. The only difference is that I will live on, she didn't. The moment I close my eyes, I imagine her lifeless cold body in front of me and me crying desperately to bring her back to life.

Much loved characters are seldom real. Much loved characters are fictional. I cried when Kamado Tanjiro[53] lost his family. I cried when Rengoku[54] died. Somehow now, Maa and Rengoku are on the same dimension of

---

[53] Kamado Tanjiro - A character (the protagonist) from Demon slayer, an anime created by Koyoharu Gotouge.

[54] Rengoku - Another character (an inspirational, allegorical figure) from Demon slayer, an anime created by Koyoharu Gotouge. He was a Hashira; a pillar of justice in the anime.

disbelief. They are both fictional. They are both non-existent. I know they exist as characters but there's no way I can ever communicate with them, no matter how much I try. I'll probably wait forever to earn another moment with Maa. I cried when Kurama[55] died. I felt like a part of me was systematically removed. The whole fandom cried when Kurama died. I almost feel like Naruto looking up desperately at the sky as Kurama wishes him goodbye for the last time. He grew up without parents but with Kurama and I grew up with Maa and Baba. Losing Maa is nothing less than Naruto losing Kurama. I cried when Jiraiya[56] died and I cried my heart out multiple times. I also cried when Vegeta[57] died while sacrificing himself in order to defeat Majin Buu.

When Maa died, I turned into a stone. I broke down a couple of times and I cried but I didn't undergo catharsis.

---

[55] Kurama – A character from Naruto, the anime and Manga by Masashi Kishimoto. Kurama, once the demon fox who made Naruto the nine-tail Jinchuriki, once feared, became the friend Naruto needed to be the protagonist in this Shonen (Bildungsroman) anime.

[56] Jiraiya – A legendary Sannin from the anime and manga Naruto by Masashi Kishimoto. He was the mentor for Naruto and the pervy sage who was much loved. Jiraiya was also the mentor of Naruto's father, the yellow flash of Konoha – Minato.

[57] Vegeta – The deuterogonist and at one time antagonist of the famous anime and Manga Dragon Ball Z.

Day 12

I can't pretend to be fine anymore

It's been twelve days since I've last seen Maa and have known that it would be the last time I was seeing her. Last night I dreamt about Maa. She used to sit in the old white plastic chair in a particular way and talk to everyone. She used to sit with her back towards one handle and sit with her legs up on another handle, like on a hammock. I was seated opposite to her in the exact same fashion and we were talking about something. She suddenly portrayed her disbelief of the situation with a vehement head shake saying no, and that's when my mind realised that it was a dream. My eyes opened. I realised I was in the bed, alone, away from home. I looked at my phone and it was 3 am. I tried going back to sleep but thoughts kept creeping into my mind. I kept thinking about Maa till I felt tired and slept off when, I don't know.

This morning I suddenly noticed that the plants at the place I put up are all dying. There has been a severe shortage of water and no one felt like watering the plants. I immediately collected some water and watered the plants. Somehow watering the plants was my way of a subtle homage to Maa. Maa loved plants after all. I sat down there, on the swing chair and kept staring at the plants, sky and everything around me. I kept looking blankly at everything. I suddenly don't feel the need to emote as much. The compulsory smile, the head nod, the accepting shoulder and head sideways tug and the unfrowned forehead happiness, all signs of paralingual communication[58], now seem like distant needs for me. I smile only when I genuinely want to. I don't look if I don't need to, I don't talk if I don't want to. Robotic, in some terms, but this keeps me cocooned. I was socially outgoing, now I'm hating social interactions other than ones which involve people I want around me. It's very awkward, but this is what it is.

I remember walking out of the room where Maa's lifeless body was kept. I suddenly had this intention to walk away from her dead body. The reason I called her Maa was because of both physical and non-physical reasons and her not responding or talking to me meant that I didn't need to wait anymore. This sudden incoming wave of rationalism forced me to ask everyone to take her away to the burning ghat. I wanted it to get over as quickly as possible and I did not want it to get delayed. I wanted it to get over and I wanted to quickly repress it. I was mostly calm. Tuli was so hurt that she almost could not breathe. Amma was beating herself up and crying. Baba broke down. Kaku

---

[58] Paralingual communication – A lot of communication happens beyond just speech. There is a lot of information being conveyed through the pitch variations in speech, the facial expressions and the hand or body movements. While speech is lingual communication, the rest is paralingual communication.

was crying. Tua curled herself up in a ball, hugged me and cried. I just ran my hands down her face and I wish she opened her eyes to speak to me, once again. I wish she did. It is now that I almost cannot see, while I write this. This takes me back to the enormous baggage I have been carrying around, pretending like it's a part of life. I can't stop crying as I write this. I can't pretend anymore. I can't pretend like death is normal. I can't pretend like I don't need Maa anymore. I can't pretend like I don't miss her. I can't keep telling people that Maa is no more and it hurts telling people that she is no more. I can't pretend to be fine anymore. My world has suddenly stopped existing and I am not okay. Tomorrow morning, these tears will not flow down my cheeks anymore. Tomorrow morning, I'll wear a fresh facade of happiness and normalcy when I go to the university and no one will understand a thing. Tomorrow morning, people will ask me what happened and how she died. I'll be ready. I know I will.

But I know, when I come back after the day, and it will be time when Maa used to call, the doors to that repressed memory will once again be opened and I'll cry alone again. It'll be an abyss that will never be filled again. Alone, in this room, devoid of human contact, I can emote.

This evening when I was cycling through the colony, the subtle interplay between the street lights and the tree leaves brought about a mystical demeanour to the lonely streets. There were patches of yellowish white light flickering through the leaves of the huge trees. The crunching of dry leaves under the tyres of the bicycle made a noise that scared away the dogs idlying on the road. Suddenly I smelled the beautiful aroma of "Bell phul" (Arabian Jasmine) in the air

It immediately teleported me back twenty five years back. Maa used to take me to Mamabari, once a week. I remember asking Maa what flowers those were, which greeted the entrance of Mamabari. They were little white flowers which had two layers of five petals each on them. I plucked a couple of them and kept them in my pocket. They smelled like delicacies to my olfactory senses and I just could not have enough of them. Maa looked flustered and stared into my eyes. Her expression then changed to somewhat of subtle grief and she told me that there were innumerable flowers on the ground. I didn't need to pluck them off the tree. I felt bad, I remember. I hated Maa crying or not being fine. I just wanted her to be fine at all times. I've never plucked another flower in my life again. I've collected a lot of flowers with Maa, but never plucked one. And yet, the most beautiful flower I ever saw was plucked right from me, before the flower fell of its own accord. Some things are unexplainable and inexplicably complicated. By the time I was done playing this memory in my mind, I was almost teary. I have so many memories with Maa that this book will not do justice to those. I keep hopping between memories of Maa. These days, I've been less in the present and more in the past, still living happily ever after with Maa, undead. I guess those repressed memories have been giving me hypnic jerks while I sleep. I guess that's why I've been seeing a lot of dreams about Maa. Maybe that's why I suddenly wake up in the middle of the night and imagine Maa speaking to me. Maybe that's why I keep on wishing that Maa never died. My mind has made incidents suit itself. Whenever I think of Maa, I almost deliberately remove the memories of 22 March 2022. I always skip back to the time I was last home, in January. I spent the whole month with everyone at home, specially Maa and it just feels like yesterday. Maybe that is why, I'm still in denial and believe that Maa will text me, call me and I'll hear her voice again.

Day 13

There's a smell of false
spontaneity to everything

It's been thirteen days since I've been repressing memories of Maa, avoiding looking at her pictures and avoiding every emotion that has to do with her. It's been thirteen days since I've almost categorically avoided human contact to a huge extent, been cast into a deep depression and have almost given up on pretend smiling. It's also been thirteen days since I've realised that in spite of having had an amazing life, a life of service to everyone, you might not get that back for yourself. The world went on like nothing happened. I feel like I belong to a parallel dimension where things drastically changed. I feel like I've been dragged into a black hole, noodlefied[59] and then dragged behind the event horizon before I realised what

---

[59] Noodlefied – An effect which one would notice when entering head on into a black hole, through the event horizon. Due to the strong gravitational forces working in a black hole, the part of a person closest to the black hole would be elongated till it tears into two. The process repeats till the person or object is transformed into a stream of atoms; then quarks or whatever is smaller than that in the quantum realm.

happened. I guess it would be better and for science, had that happened instead of Maa having to die.

I keep on looking at the streets and colonies around me and there's a smell of false spontaneity to everything. The hedges being trimmed after being systematically uprooted from their actual niches would be a good example to start with. The need to deforest massive forests for civilisation to breach through nature's heart and then planting a couple of trees at the road side and calling it a day, would be another good example. The need for the yearly or quarterly trimming of plants in pots at home is another of those unbelievable ideas we believe in. We have a strange sense of beauty away from actual beauty. We believe in existence the way we think it is and not the way it always has been. We uproot forests to make way for amazing technological advancements and yet in the process forget to give back what we destroyed. Maa never loved trees or plants being trimmed. She even fought with Baba when he took initiative to trim a few trees at home. Maa didn't believe in these falsified propagandas of Fibonaccian[60] beauty. Granted that she did purchase a lot of plants, in a way digging her way through the capitalist system but she let her plants grow, the way they would be at their natural origins. I understand there's a huge dilemma of plants being removed from their original places here but my point is that the irony of nature being civilized into political societies is what kills nature in the first place.

---

[60] Fibonacci – Italian mathematician

I was in the cab to my work place, the university, when I first noticed those wild yellow sunflowers. They looked beautiful. No one cared for them and no one would look back at them but Maa would have. Maa loved flowers, no matter how non-commercialised they were. Maa just loved beautiful flowers without the need for them to be expensive and shoppable. She planted plants and trees without the need for flowery validation. Yes, she loved flowers but her need for validation in a season and then being fine with the plant dying thereafter, did not exist. That taught me a thing or two about both, plants and expectations.

I sat down in the faculty lounge. There's this massive window in front of me, which opens up to a beautiful view of the Aravallis[61] and one can see beautiful ancient mountains along with fauna in variety. I came back from home after thirteen days and now I'm back to the old rushed life, away from the place I saw Maa dead and away from the people I call family. This morning when I looked out of the window, I saw something Maa wanted to see for a long time. I regret her not being there with me to see that sight. I regret Maa not being able to live, to love the magnificent beauty of the Lilac violet Jacaranda trees at the campus. A couple of months back, Maa ordered a packet of Jacaranda tree seeds from somewhere and she wanted to plant those seeds everywhere in our city. Lately our city has been made into a civilised mess. Our city has

---

[61] Aravalli – one of the most ancient mountain ranges in the world; located in Northern India

seen a lot of tall buildings being built and an even larger number of trees being killed in the process. No one cares if a plant is killed in the process of building a building. Maa cried when after Amphan[62], the cyclone, hundreds of ancient trees were uprooted in the city and the civic authorities just cut them away and called it a day. They took no initiatives to replant or replenish. Maa cried when the huge trees in the cemetery in front of our house fell down in Amphan. She knew she would not be able to watch birds anymore. The trees, the shelters for beautiful birds were gone and she would not be able to see amazing birds sitting at the terrace anymore. Maa cried when Dadu suddenly cut all the trees and saplings in our home, in order to make way for a new room. Maa felt bad. She was one with nature. It was almost as if she could empathize with nature. Today when I saw the pots dry to the bone and devoid of water I felt bad. The plants were drooping and a few had died. Somewhere, it feels like Maa is pushing me to carry her torch ahead as if I have partially inculcated that value from her.

There's this immaculate feeling of completeness when I go to the hills, like I have been united with a long lost love of my life, like I've gotten a whiff of fresh air after being suffocated for long inside a thick cheap plastic. It's like I know I'm going to die if I'm inside the plastic and I want to burst out of that plastic bubble. Going to the hills make me feel like I've attained Nirvana. Maa used to feel the

---

[62] Amphan – a storm which happened in 2020 in the Eastern Coast of India. It wreaked a lot of havoc.

same. That's probably why they say birds of the same feather flock together. Maa was suffocated and hypoxic when they all reached Sandakfu. Maa didn't know it would be her last trip. Maa didn't realise she would leave her home for the last time, walking and come back on a stretcher, dead! Maa didn't realise she would never come back. She kept all her cloths, unfolded, on the bed. She left all her documents, dishevelled, in the drawers.

She left all ornaments, purchased for our wedding, in an old bag of mine and shoved it into an old almirah. She wasn't ready. It's as if, she was suffocated in the plastic bag and she desperately wanted an out. She never realised, she would never come back to fold her cloths, organise her drawer and hand over the ornaments to Tulika. She never realised she would die in the process of going to a place, which she thought would give her relief. I didn't want Maa and Baba to go to Sandakfu. I wanted them to come over to my place. I wanted them to stay at my place for a couple of days. I promised them, I would take them to Sattal, a beautiful lake hidden in the lower Himalayas. We have been there before and Maa loved the birds and trees there. I realise that, had I forced them to come here, I would probably still be waiting for her call now, at 9.50pm. I would still be waiting to talk to her over video call and I would still be waiting for Maa Baba and Tua to come visit me in May. May will come. Baba and Tua will come but Maa will never come again. I'll never see her again. I realise that if I had forced them to come stay with me, Maa would not have to go through an agonizing and tormenting pain before finally dying. She would not have to go through multiple organ failure due to hypoxia and then be wrongly diagnosed or not be diagnosed at all, be transferred to her friends in Kolkata from Siliguri, only to die fifty odd kilometres from the place which we thought would save her. She didn't make it. Baba regrets every decision he has made. Baba regrets not bringing Maa and Tua to my place. Baba blames himself but he's not responsible. He did his best to keep Maa happy when she lived. Blaming oneself for the choices and decisions he has made because she is no more, doesn't change a thing and moreover he wasn't wrong! Probably in a parallel universe, in a disconnected string, Maa is still alive and I'm still waiting for her call. I'm still waiting for her to give me a call and smile at my face, ask me if I've had dinner, ask me to tell her what's going on in my life and share her day's story. Probably in another parallel universe I'm waiting at home for her to return from her workplace after having delivered a couple of babies, shown them the light for the first time. Perhaps in another parallel universe Maa is at home after a traumatic one week at the hospital where she was rightly diagnosed, out under intensive treatment and cured of the root cause. That version of her would have lived through our wedding and she would be in all the pics of our wedding. She would have been be there right beside me, smiling, photobombing and hugging both of us while still shouting at Tua for not wearing her braces (my sister hates wearing her braces). The piercing and stabbing pain I have to encounter every time I think about how she had to go through extreme pain before she died, numbs me and I fail to respond with any sensible emotions. Perhaps in another stringed bubbled universe, I am absolutely coherent and still have someone to call Maa. Perhaps if I had the interdimensional gun portal from Rick[63], I would have made it into another stringed universe. I would have gotten things right. I wish I was Morty and I had a Rick!

When I was going around the block this evening on my cycle, I saw an young couple walking their baby in a pram. Both of them smiled at each other while they kept talking about, what I could hear in a jiffy, about how their baby is quickly growing up and soon they will be called Papa and Mumma. Being with a person through thick and thin, for forty two years and then suddenly having to live the rest of your life without the presence of the person you called your wife, your soulmate and the person you did everything for, for forty two years is just outright terrorising. I can't even start to understand the variety of emotions one has to go through in such a long time. Baba keeps on texting me that he feels like he has lost. Baba keeps on silently crying when he's alone. Baba calls me and keeps talking to me like a man who has already condemned himself to oblivion, instead of living his life out. That's what Maa would have wanted, for Baba to live his life with dignity, honour and with no regrets. Baba keeps on talking to me about his death and how it would unite him with Maa. I fail to understand how Baba, a man of science suddenly fell prey to the belief of afterlife. I fail to understand how Baba, doesn't get that once a body has been burnt, it just stops to exist and there's nothing you

---

[63] Rick – The beloved character Rick Sanchez and Morty Smith are from the series Rick and Morty on Netflix; created by Justin Roiland and Dan Harmon.

can do to reunite with them, whatsoever. But I can't blame him. We humans have been displacing, using language for millennia now trying to rationalise everything we think are unwanted elements in life, like say, death. We have created tall tales of afterlife, rebirth, reincarnation and soul transfer, in different cultures respectively. We humans have also, first, delved into the idea of love and family. We have delved into a system which feeds into the need for validation on our parts. We have dived deep into a system which forbids us to be singular islands of DNA. We have decorated and emblazoned the whole process of choosing a mate, getting to know them before we reproduce with them. We have rationalised the fact that you're going to share DNA with someone in order to get another 23 pairs of chromosomes from them, to create an offspring through a set of displaced rituals, we call a marriage. Not only that but we have also rationalised Gods and devils, humans and angels. We have rationalised the death of people who have died at old age by saying that they were probably suffering and I have rationalised Maa's sudden death by saying that she was suffering the last one week, before she died. The problem arises when we tend to deconstruct the onion like layers. We start realising that the story we are creating makes sense to us, only because we are relying on the apparent structures which we think, give us solidarity and strength. I start to crumble the moment I realise that Maa had an amazing life and she did not deserve those last seven days. I start to break down the moment I realise, she was not ready to die. I break down when I realise I'll never speak to her again, never hug her again, never sleep in her lap again and never lie down beside her again. She will never call out my name again. She will never tell me stories again or never call me again. She will never wake me up in the morning to show me something amazing or ask me to sleep at night because it's late. She's gone. A husk of memories remain till we last. The last of her memories will be gone the moment, the people who loved her the most, would be gone.

Day 14

Two weeks later

It's been two weeks since Maa left us all due to the sheer carelessness of corporate medicine. I woke up on the morning of 22 March, expecting to see the person I love the most, as soon as I reached Kolkata from Gurgaon. Baba asked me to get a ticket to Kolkata and not Siliguri since they were already bringing Maa to Kolkata. Little did he know that Maa would succumb to the multi organ failure which was induced by hypoxia at high altitude. When I had slept, the night before Baba got me to speak to Maa and that was the last time I spoke to her, ever! Baba told me that she was in pain but she was stable. She had an elevated pulse rate but she would be fine. Next morning, I boarded my cab, happy, yet uncomfortable and I got mentally ready to meet Maa. When I was in the cab I called Baba to know about the whereabouts then and when they would reach Kolkata, but he didn't take my call. A sudden chill ran down my spine as if it meant something. I called Kaku and he picked up my call. He said that they were at Ranaghat. Maa had suddenly gone into cardiac arrest and she was not breathing. Luckily there was a hospital exactly hundred metres away and they intubed her, put her into complete ventilation. Maa was in critical condition, he said and he was almost in tears. I never heard him cry. This was the first time in the last five days that I heard him hopeless. "Is there nothing we can do?", I asked almost powerlessly. He said the resident medical officer was doing everything to save Maa. It was 4.40 am then. I disconnected the phone, almost in a daze. I went into autopilot and I don't exactly remember what happened in the next one hour. I don't remember when I reached the airport or when I checked in, when I sat at the airport boarding gate and so on. I just wanted Maa to be fine. I just wanted Maa to endure. I wanted Maa to survive, so that I could still be with her, speak to her, hug her, converse about the world with her and travel with her. I called Baba from the boarding gate and his phone was switched off. I realised the journey was long and his phone might have died. I called Kaku and his phone was switched off. I called the others accompanying Baba and Kaku and their phones were switched off. This was when I could induce a pattern in this subtle yet understandable behaviour. I realised something was really wrong. I couldn't control my tears. I could see flashes of Maa and my life I have spent with her. I could suddenly not control my tears anymore. I was frozen, stuck and couldn't breathe. No one would give me closure, as to what happened. No one picked up my call. I remember walking into the flight and taking my seat. This time I didn't call the ones I called before. I called uncle, Tuli's Baba since I knew he was also there. My call was received and he sounded normal. For a split second I thought I was being afraid of nothing. He asked me whether I boarded the flight to which I said, I did. He then asked me to talk to Baba. Baba took the call, asked me the same thing and then suddenly broke down, as if he was pretending that

Catharsis with Maa

things were normal; as if the act of normalcy was too hard for him at that point in time. "Khub kharap condition Maa er Babui. Amar khub bhoy lagche" (Maa is in critical condition Babui. I'm frightened). I just responded saying I'll be there with all of them soon and to keep her safe. The phone disconnected. The transient state of peace after talking to Kaku was over. I was once again embroiled in a wave of deduction. While my mind somehow kept telling me that Maa was gone, my mind kept telling me she wasn't. I didn't get closure. No one told me she was dead. No one gave me closure. Maa was still Schrodinger's cat all over again. I couldn't help crying helplessly by myself while everyone in the flight kept looking at me. I kept imagining what life would be without Maa and couldn't help being frightened about the inevitable but kept on questioning what exactly went wrong. She was stable till the time I had gone to sleep the night before, or at least that is what I thought. All throughout the flight I broke down multiple times and I blacked out because I was tired of thinking multiple times. When the flight finally landed, I called Kaku and asked them where they are. Kaku said they are at Ranaghat and that Tua and my other siblings would come to receive me at the airport. When I boarded our car after leaving the airport, I sat down and couldn't gather the courage to ask about an update. I was afraid I would be told about the inevitable.

What happened after this is something I'll never forget. I got a call from Kaku saying that I'm being taken home, not to Ranaghat and they are returning. That was the moment, Maa was no longer in Schrodinger's box but out of it. The state of inability to understand was over. I knew what it was then. I broke down once again and Tua hugged me and cried. We were almost inconsolable. My brother, who lost his father (my uncle) last year went through a similar time and he was there. I'm sure he tried to console me but I just couldn't agree with what was happening. Tua asked me, "Who told you? Did my father tell you now?".

I actually didn't know it. Circumstantial evidence and syntactic cues, along with the way people were behaving since 4.40am with me, prompted to only one thing. Maa was gone. I didn't want closure. I wanted her. I wanted her to be alive and breathing. I wanted her to live on. I wanted her to talk to me and tell me things.

I kept wondering if she is still alive and that they are probably bringing her back healthy and under medication. No one still told me what happened. I saw my sister cry for the first time. She never cries. She's as strong as a carbon fibre diamond hybrid. She cried that day. I kept believing she was alive.

I remember getting Neha's[64] text asking me how Maa was. I couldn't reply to her because I didn't want to believe it myself. I wanted to respond to her only when I knew what was in the box. Everyone knew that Maa was hospitalised and everyone was sure she would be back home soon, safe and sound.

---

[64] Neha – a friend of the author

Catharsis with Maa

I remember reaching home and I didn't realise when I reached home. There was a huge gathering of people in front of home. I deboarded the car and went straight inside. I kept my bag in Amma's room and as if to ask where Maa is, I gestured at someone who was in front of me. They pointed towards the guest room. And there she was, safe and sound, sleeping her eternal sleep, under a mattress of flowers, unable to see her son, in shock, to see her like that. There she lied, with no expressions on her face but with petals on her eyes, vermillion on her forehead and commercialised flowers on her, tube roses. She lied there unconscious and oblivious of what was going on beside her. She lied there, cold, lifeless, emotionless, expressionless, speechless, dead! She was no longer in Schrodinger's box. Maa was actually gone. I slowly sat down. I couldn't feel my body. I still couldn't believe that she was in front of me, but she wasn't there. I couldn't believe that thirty one years of memories lied dead in front of me. I couldn't believe that thirty one years of unending conversations, bonding, incomparable and unconditional love, hugs and kisses, fights and makeups, travelogues, videos and pictures, selfies, teachings and preaching, all lied in front of me and all I could do was swallow my feelings, look at her face with smudgy eyes and accept reality. I kept sobbing inconsolably as I sat down beside her, slowly moving my hands towards her face. I extended one finger and touched her body. It was cold. It didn't have Maa's warmth. I ran my fingers down her cheeks, then her hair, then her forehead and then her eyes. She didn't respond. I spoke to her softly. "Why Maa why?", I asked. She didn't respond. I slowly held her hand and they were cold. Whenever I would extend my hands towards Maa she would hold my hand back and grab my fingers, adore me. She didn't anymore. Her hands were still, cold and non-responsive. She didn't recognise her son, she loved more than herself and wanted to see get married to the love of his life, in December. She died before knowing her son will eventually get married. She died before experiencing the beauty and magnanimity of the flowers blooming that day. She died way before she was supposed to. I wasn't ready. We weren't ready. We still aren't. Why Maa? Why?

It's hard to believe that the person I love the most was struggling for her life and gasping for air, desperately trying to breathe, helplessly trying to pump blood with her as arrested heart, trying to live because, who doesn't want to live? It's hard to believe that Maa was dead when I was in the airport, checking in. It's hard to imagine that Maa was gone, long before I realised she was gone. I regret not being able to see her the last time. I'll have to live with it. Why Maa? Why?

I have this subtle feeling of incompleteness all the time. Maa wasn't a part of my life when I was here, in Gurgaon. Maa wasn't here when I woke up in the morning or got ready or went to work or worked or when I came back or when I rested in the evening or when I went to play table tennis downstairs or when I had dinner and when I went back to sleep after a few hours of watching television. Maa was not there. Her not existing should practically not change anything except for a few phone calls, video calls, texts. Her not being there should make home visits less exciting, sad. Her not being at home would mean the dogs would have one less person to feed them. Her not being there would mean one less doctor to care for patients the way she did, irrespective of the social status of the patient. Her not existing in flesh would mean our family would have one less member to feed and worry about but the other members would inadvertently need to fend for themselves since the doctor in the family doesn't exist anymore. Her not being alive anymore would mean one less person would care about plants, one less person would care about birds and their habitats. Her not existing would mean I would get less opportunities to travel with her and travel in general. Her not living would mean one less person would donate to charity.

We humans have made up a world for ourselves where our social structure is so symbolic, symbolic in the Saussurian sense of the term, as well as Charles Saunders Pierce point of view that parents have been put up on a pedestal so high that it's almost impossible to recover from a shock of missing and losing them. That signified concept is way beyond the reach of simpler concept like 'get over it' or 'forget'. We have covered the concept of genetic or biological parents in an onion like covering of love and family with multiple safeguards by society such that bonds like this remain in the top tier of the sociological ladder. Such bonds are the celestial, ethereal level of bonds.

Day 15

My eyes opened and there
I was, still on my bed

Fifteen days and I still cry like a baby, every time I miss Maa. Fifteen days and I still can't get over the fact that Maa is gone. Fifteen days and I can still hear Maa everywhere. I can still hear the echoes of her voice everywhere. I guess I was fresh out of rem sleep when I suddenly heard Maa speak to me. For a few seconds I went back fifteen days back when Maa's melody was still a part of my symphony. For a few seconds, my brain subconsciously lateralized the information and localised it such that it can prepare a response to reply to Maa. Maa said, "Uthey por. Atta baaje!" (Get up Tatai. It's 8am). Alas, life had other plans for me. The moment I opened my eyes, I was brought back to the lonely bed in Gurgaon, making me mentally and physically come back to the stark reality that is now. I realised that my brain was just trying to create a myth, which is a paradox. My brain was trying to create an alternate truth to give me a silver lining of closure, happiness or anything related. I almost felt like someone tore my heart out, when I heard Maa's voice and then almost instantaneously had to make my brain believe that I needed to unhear her voice, I heard then, because it wasn't real. It's very difficult to accept the fact that it was not her voice but rather a figment of my imagination. Maa's voice is everywhere. Maa isn't.

Last night, my eyes suddenly opened around 3 am and I think I was awake when it happened again. I turned to the side and I could hear Maa breathe. She had this faint snore to her sleep breathing and I could clearly hear it. I turned towards her and tried to put my hands on hers and that's when my eyes really opened. There was nothing! What I could see was simply put, darkness! The room would be at the max, at 1 Lux of brightness and what I could see was a pillow next to me, my spectacles, my mobile phone and a bedsheet. Maa wasn't there. What's happening to me? All of a sudden, the air conditioner started to act up and the room was uncomfortable; very uncomfortable. It started to burn my eyes and my body. I was stuck. I couldn't move my body. I tried to move my body and get up but I couldn't. I just couldn't move. I tried to even move a finger and I realised I was paralyzed. I just couldn't move. I tried to look at the air conditioner once again and all I could see was a blue blur, induced by the blue led on it. I suddenly felt out of breath, suffocated and cornered. I felt claustrophobic and I wanted, desperately to go out for a fresh breath of air. It felt like someone placed a couple of hundred kilograms of weight on me and I just couldn't shake the weights off. I tried and tried but I just couldn't. I could eventually not hear the fan, the air conditioner and the sound of my breathing. Every sound, every sight was slowly moving away from me. The room suddenly turned extremely dark. I could not see the led anymore. The sensation of me feeling hot, also seemed to move away. As things started to change even further, I suddenly couldn't breathe anymore. I gasped for air but I just couldn't breathe. As I kept gasping for air, I felt like I was drowning, slowly but surely in some sort of dense and viscous liquid. I was drowning in it. I was dying...

My eyes opened and there I was, still on my bed. There was a faint light from the early morning sun. Through the little gap in the curtains, I could see a bluish tinge in the sky. I slowly turned towards the window and I realised I was dreaming. Maa wasn't breathing beside me nor was I drowning. The air conditioner was on, all along and I was covered in a bedsheet, half folded, as if someone covered me in a hurry. The pillow did lie beside me, as if someone got up in a hurry, but no one was lying beside me. I was truly alone in the room. That was a dream, a dream suggests my mental condition after Maa's death. I just cannot get over her death.

Baba called me on the evening of 16 March. I didn't have my phone and I was using Neha's phone. Baba called me and hindered. He then told me that he had to admit Maa to a hospital due to acute breathing problems, due to altitude sickness. That day I had hope that I would see Maa soon. That day I was hopeful that it was only temporary and that Maa would be stable soon, ready to get on with her life. Baba sounded pretty confident Maa would be fine. I was confident because he was. From there to now, when Maa is just the remnant of a myth in my life, 'mother' it's been a long couple of nights, I cried my way through. From there to now, Maa has come a long way from being a person who can only be described as a person who is extremely joyous, happy go lucky, extremely energetic and magnanimous to just a couple of pictures, voice notes, videos and teary eyes.

The first day I reached office after I came back from home after Maa left us all, I could not bear the sight of a picture Tulika gifted Maa. It was on my work table. It was a picture of me, Maa and Tulika at Bheemtal framed on a wooden frame. It was on my table. Today I gathered the courage to pick it up and look at it. Maa looked beautiful, so did Tulika. We were on the way to Sattal. Maa had asked me to take her to Sattal because she wanted to engage in birdwatching. Had I forced Maa and Baba to come to me, we would probably be bird watching in Sattal now, instead of me writing a journaled account of how I am dealing with Maa's death. It doesn't end. I thought eventually things would be easier. I thought eventually I would be fine but I just can't shake the feeling that, things will never be the same again. I keep trying to keep myself engaged, so that I don't remember Maa is gone but she was my Maa. We have literally done everything together, at one point in time or the other. There is nothing I can do in life right now, that would not remind me of Maa. There's nothing that can suddenly give me extreme strength other than the radical rationalism I believe in some times. In spite of everything, my eyes moisten up once in a while and sometimes I break into fits of uncontrollable tears. I keep crying till I cannot breathe and then suddenly I just turn into a block of stone, devoid of feelings. Thereafter, my facial expressions change to that of extreme calm and I suddenly do not harbour or let discern any sort of facial expression. It is then that I successfully repress the thoughts which are on my mind and successfully clear my thoughts about Maa. Deep within there's a huge lake of emotions lurking beneath the surface. Deep within me, there are emotions and facts I do not want to deal with now. Deep within me, I'm broken. Deep within me, I miss Maa. Deep within me, I know I'll never see her again and yet here I am still trying to build a mythical string universe where the alternate reality is so amusing that I sometimes fail to realise which ontological reality I am a part of. I forget my actual reality and tend to skip over to a different reality I want to be a part of, rather than the reality I already am, a part of. I don't know which of the stages of grief I'm at, amongst the five stages of grief that are mostly referred to because sometimes I don't even know I'm grieving . I know I'll never be privy to Maa's loving self again, but all I can say is, I miss her, a lot; a hell lot. I feel cold, cold from the amount of death I've experienced in the last couple of days. Maa's leaving has left me spellbound, silent, cold and stoned. I kept on trying to cope with her death and soon enough I couldn't sleep at night. Soon enough I couldn't stop myself from crying till I gasped for air and then suddenly stopped like someone had pressed a button on me. Maa's death has left me unprepared, bewildered and questioning. Maa's death has left me in deep denial. Maa's death was not needed. She had time, at least that's what we all thought. It wasn't her time. We weren't ready. I still am not. I still imagine Maa to appear, in front of me, suddenly and stay forever.

Day 17

*I can feel the paradigmatic exigencies
changing around me*

I can never forget the last conversation I've had with her. It's been seventeen days and even though I've been thinking about Maa on and off, I'm starting to realise that I'm desperately trying to speak to her, hear her voice. I keep hearing her here and there and I end up playing her last conversation in my mind where she kept saying how much pain she was in. I keep going back to her last conversation when she still believed she would see me and grab me in her arms. I still keep going back to her last conversation when I knew I would see her in another ten hours. I just didn't realise I wouldn't see her alive. It doesn't matter if I'm in a crowd or in a deserted place. The moment I do something, I inadvertently keep reverting to thinking about Maa and how she would have reacted to this, had she been there and how she would have spent time with me. Baba tries to hide his pain but in the end Baba can't hide his tears. But even though he's shattered, he keeps trying to recentre his life and mine. We are left to survive the woman we loved the most. We are left to fend for each other, while the woman who did everything to keep us safe and alive is gone.

We humans are feeble and we tend to find excuses to everything. From the day Maa died, I have been playing back all events that led to her death and I keep trying to pin the blame on someone or the other, with no avail. I keep on trying to find out, what went wrong and why she died, with no result. I keep trying to suddenly find a justification for her death but all I find are incomplete reasons. To this date, in an age of medical exploration and victory, no sound explanation for Maa's death was found and I doubt a sound explanation will ever be found. I keep looking for an instance to seek closure but I will never find any. I keep on waking up in the middle of the night, tired of my thoughts and I cry myself back to sleep, once I'm in the stoned state again. I fail to understand, how, in a world where victims with their complete limbs severed survive accidents, where a patient in their eighties survives cancer, where a person survives after an otherwise fatal crash, where a person survives a fall from the sixth floor, where a person gets eaten by a titan and lives with a magical miraculous transformation, but a doctor with severe hypoxia dies without proper diagnosis and prognosis. I keep trying to find a reason why Maa died in an age of technology, science and medicine with improved life expectancy. I fail to understand why!

Everybody leaves someday. Once happy and joyous families, brimming with happiness, hugs, tears, joys, quarrels and parties, eventually turn into an empire of dust. While the concrete husks which once housed beautiful memories keep standing on the tired shreds of Gaia, oblivion eventually grabs its share of those sheds of skins. Starting with the eldest to the youngest or in some misdemeanoured situation like Maa, from the most unfortunate to the fortunate, everybody dies. And as the last person in the family dies, their little tightly knit society, their photographs, their ideas, their love for each other, their stories, their little memories, their idiolects, their way of talking to each other, the first words of children in their family, the last uttered sentences by family members, the food they loved the most and cooked the worst, the songs that were played, the plants that adorned the family, the pictures that emblazoned their walls, the places they visited together, the losses they faced together and the victories they garnered together, all fades away into an ever ravaging stream of time's ravaging.

What remains of them are just the materials that haven't decomposed yet, the husk of a house they lived in, the bricks in it and the plants that once were loved and cared for. Their home dies. It hurts. My patience is dwindling. And as I hold on to the last lees of my syntagmatic[65] existence, Maa, and her memories and as I desperately keep fighting to hold on to everything that keeps her alive for me, I can feel the paradigmatic[66] exigencies changing around me.

---

[65] Syntagmatic – a system of signs propounded by Ferdinand de Saussure claiming that most structures in language first follow a set of rules that are rigid followed by choices we call paradigms

[66] Paradigms – choices we make after following syntagms

I know that it won't be long before everyone will probably forget 22 March. I will forget? I do not know, honestly. I will probably just learn to live in this diachronicity by accepting to live within the synchronicity.

Of Indelible Pains and Endless Cacophony

The last few minutes

There's a certain kind of indelible pain from the moment when Maa was lying there lifeless at the burning ghat, adorned by flowers and now conscious relatives concerned about our family, in a sea of cacophony, tears, bird sounds and the silent whooshing of the holy Ganges. As her only son, I was responsible for lighting her pyre on fire; or was I? Maa never differentiated between Tua and me. She was as much a daughter to Maa as I'm a son to her. I looked at the relatives looking at me to end the commotion, as if the lighting of the fire would end all pains. I couldn't get myself to look at Maa's lifeless corpse, looking almost as if she was looking at me through the petals of flowers, begging me to end this madness. I faintly remember someone holding me hand and entrusting a wooden torch to my hand. I was supposed to fake-lit her face on fire, post which the body is generally taken to the electric pyre, where it is burnt. I quickly turned to Tua and to Tulika, as if masquerading my painful face in an act of strength for their touch; grabbed their hands and held their hands in mine. Many others quickly followed suit and soon, we were revolving around her body in circles. It is a ritual for the departed, allowing them safe passage into the afterlife, a belief I don't believe in. Kaku, as if to advise, told us that there was no need to light her face on fire if we didn't want to; the hands were good enough. I remember, not looking at her body, as I kept rotating around her. Yes, I still refer to Maa, then dead, as 'her' because she was still a planet in herself, probably like the old Mars, lying there, lifeless. I remember deliberately avoiding looking at her. As the ritual was done, people started to pick up her body, then laid out on a piece of cheap wooden framework. I knew it was time. It would be Moments before Maa in her corporal form would finally be gone. It was Moments before I would never see her again. My whole life started to play in front of my eyes; the way she cared for me, the way she loved us all, the way she nagged about things, the fervour with which she identified and showed me flora and fauna; everything would be gone in Moments. I kept holding on to a piece of wood, as the others kept taking her body to the electric pyre. And soon, after climbing a long flight of stairs, there it was, the furnace. This was goodbye, the final goodbye. With dulled eyes and a translucent layer of tears, I looked at Maa and broke down one last time before her body would be seen no more. I held her hands. I embraced her. I kissed her forehead one last time and I looked at the others, as if to signal them to do what was needed. Someone grabbed me from behind and pulled me back. The furnace was hot, extremely hot. They pushed her body inside. Her face looked red in the glow of the furnace and I could smell her cloths starting to burn. The furnace gate was closed, as if to end an era! The furnace gate closed, as if to signal for us, the final goodbye; as if it was the end of some grand act. The curtain dropped after the final scene, final act.

As I walked out of the furnace room, Tua grabbed onto me and we walked out slowly and unsure footed. This was when I realised she was actually gone. Baba stood at one corner, crying and all I could do was embrace him. I had no words to console him for our loss. I had nothing that would replace his loss. Nothing ever will. As we walked out, I imagined her body slowly burning, limb by limb, muscle by muscle, bone by bone. And as the whole process of transfer of energy, conservation of energy or whatever convenient we can call it, happened, I kept looking at the flow of time, visible in the ripples of river Ganges. There was this certain calmness to the way the water flowed, not caring about what happened elsewhere, not bothered about the hue and cry of the world around it, oblivious to everything around it. I yearned to be the water, oblivious of emotions, pain and suffering but alas, a human fails to reach those standards of coldness, until dead.

I always knew this would happen. I knew Maa would die someday, so will we all. I wasn't just ready for it to happen so soon, so early. I wasn't ready for all I had invested in Maa, to be gone to waste so soon. I knew someday she would die and I would have to live with it. Now when it's happened already, I feel cold, emotionless mostly and unreactive to most things. I feel like a part of me has died along with her, leaving a shell that is otherwise functional.

Why do they have to die? Why can't we live on like the immortal jellyfishes, or the rather famous phoenix, rising from our flames? Why can't we humans live forever? Why can't we upload our consciousness to some server capable of human brain mapping and then download it to another capable body, matching our physical, environmental specs, resuming from where we left off in our previous life. Why can't we not die? Why did Maa have to die now, this early? I have no answers to any of these. I just know that the fleeting jiffy of time, we call a lifetime is what it is due to its fleetingness and subtle frailty. Forever is a drag and probably would bore us. But has anyone lived forever to have claimed such a statement? No?

Maa's Mornings

A typical morning in Maa's day

Maa used to wake up exactly around 5.30am in the morning post which she would revisit the bed once again, where I would be. She would at times ask me whether I want to go out for a refreshing walk or ride, or at times ask me whether I'd help her out to get a special plant from somewhere she noticed and spotted the day before. At times I would request her to let me sleep but at times I would wake up because I simply loved spending time with her. We have had a lot of these morning outings. We collected plants, took a lot of drone shots, bumped into known people walking at the Ganges river banks, collected plants again, ignored people we didn't want to talk to, walked and discussed life and so on. We spent a lot of time together. Perhaps, Maa's death made me loneliest in the mornings and nights. I would sleep right next to her when at home and my day would end with a video call to her when at Gurgaon or Delhi. I would wake up in the morning and be absolutely sure that Maa would be awake. I would generally walk to the terrace, when at home or when in Gurgaon or Delhi, I would just call Maa, because I would know that she would be up and awake. Now! Now I can't call anyone. I feel terribly lonely in the mornings and nights; the times when I used to speak with her, spend time with her the most. I know there are enough people in the day, to spend time with. But at night, who will caress my forehead, who will talk to me early in the morning? Who will I randomly send bird pics to and ask for the names? Who will I send plant pics to and ask for names? Who will I share the beauty of plants with? Perhaps, this is life! Perhaps moving on and living on in spite of dire situations hitting you, is life. Perhaps living without Maa is the new life, now. Perhaps being lonely in the mornings is the new life. Perhaps accepting that I'll never wake up to her voice or her call or her silently sitting and reading the morning news or her sitting beside me and doing something random while I'd wake up, will never happen again, is life!

When I was in the first standard, Maa gifted me a globe. I kept rotating it till it rolled out of its axis once in a while. I was very excited. I used it for a very long time. Way later, in 2009, when I was well into my bachelor's degree, one day I had a fight with Maa and the only thing which bore the brunt of my anger was the globe. I threw it into the wall. It broke. I kept trying to pick up the pieces, trying to refix it, but it was broken into small pieces. The globe was a cheap but what was invested in it was memories, years of teaching and her love. I broke it. Maa cried that day. I felt so bad I kept hurting myself till my arms turned blue. She turned to a side that night and kept sobbing to herself. I didn't want to talk to her because I was more angry and guilty about myself than about the fight. I didn't have the guts to talk to her. Since she's been gone, I've been remembering all these memories one by one, as if a reminder of all the things I've done to hurt her, when she was alive. One day when I was young, I learnt the word 'sadist' and I wanted to use it on someone, just like a child wants to test out their vocabulary in sentences. I called Maa a sadist, not knowing how she would react. She asked me if I knew what I was saying. She kept confirming of I knew what I was saying. I kept saying I did. In the end, she confirmed one last time and I could see her eyes, all watery. She looked at me and smiled through her tears and told me, " In spite of doing everything to bring you up, this is what you say to me". I can't start to imagine how much it would have hurt her. I cannot forgive myself enough for being over smart and calling her a sadist. Right now I realise how much of an unsadist she was. She showered me with happiness while I did so many individual things to keep on hurting her, so many times. Unforgiving, is a word, fit for the occassion. The last few years were so perfect. Maa was really my best friend. I'm a closed person. I don't necessarily share everything with anyone, not even with Maa but she wasn't. I know everything she loved, hated, wanted, was happy about and sad about. I loved spending time with her, and so did she. I bear many grudges and I can carry them for a lifetime but she wasn't one. She loved me unconditionally, every day, even after I called her a sadist. She wasn't one.

"Tora e toh amader bhobishyot re tatai. Ekhon amra korchi, joto din parchi. Ekhon toder bhabte hobe na. Porey bhabish" (You are our future Tatai. Now we are doing for you all, as long as we can. You can think about your contributions, later on). When I kept telling her how ridiculous the whole concept of feeding thousands of guests at weddings are and how much of a waste of money they are this was her response. She kept claiming that it was not a waste of money till it was something that made people happy. She can saying how much she is looking forward to our wedding, a wedding she did not know she wouldn't be able to attend. She kept planning so many things for us and spent more than money. She spent her life on it. She invested time on it. She definitely did not know she was gonna die. Hell, I would probably be married now, had I known she would not exist now. Don't I have enough things to blame me for already?

That One Time I Died

And the memories I never had from the eyes of Maa; with a hint of Tagore

Maa was special. Her language skills were beyond what we call normal. She was so well read that her reactions would seldom be sentences and emoticons and rather more of quotes from books, poems or dramas. She was so well read in Bangla, as a literature and subject that her knowledge would be used by many in proofreading, corrections and furthering documentations. I used to call her vision as 'eagles eyes'. It was scary the way she would find out errors even before we would read whole sentences. It was surprising at times. I wonder how she would react had I been the one, who died. I remember, in 2018, when I met with the accident, forever losing a part of my left knee meniscus, luckily escaping death, in the process, I didn't tell Maa. I didn't have the guts to tell Maa and Baba. While it was not my fault that it happened, it was well within reason for me to have died that day. Maa would probably get a phone call from the nearest police station, or the hospital who would declare the time of death. She would immediately turn blank, the moment she would hear it. She would enquire if they are sure it's the same person, to which the person on the other side would affirmatively say yes. Two silent drops of tears would roll down her cheeks. She would look at her phone and silently look at it in disbelief. She would call me. Some unknown person would pick up the call. She would try asking where I am to which she would be told that I'm in some body bag, in some hospital morgue. The body would be safely kept for the next 24 hours, post which it would be burnt. She would walk towards Baba and look at him.

"We need to get tickets to Delhi, now"

"What happened Rita?"

"We need to get tickets to Delhi! Now. Get them now!"

"Rita. Calm down. What happened?"

Maa would break down after saying, "Tatai ar nei" (Tatai is gone). Maa said exactly something like this when Alice died. "Tatai, Alice ar nei. Neeche aay. Ektu dekhe Jaa. Okey ektu shesh aaram ta de" (Alice is gone. Come downstairs. Help me rest her for the last time). I have just rationalised what she would have said.

And while Baba would be busy trying to get tickets and grieving, Maa's silent sobs would have by now turned into violent cries. She would by now, be scratching her pale white skin and be hurting physically. She loved me a lot more than I imagined how much one could love another. While Baba would inform others and try and get them to help out Maa would still be in a fit of unfaithful rage, denial, violent cries and cold stares. No parent wants their offspring to die before they do. The reason they reproduce is because their children would carry forward their legacy.

They would probably be in Delhi within the next six hours, at the venue of the corpse. By then Maa would be silent, cold as a corpse herself, devoid of emotions. Baba and Maa would silently enter the morgue, guided by a man. Most people in charge of morgues in India are mostly men, not because men are less frightened of dealing with dead bodies but because of the highly prevalent gender bias and gender roles we follow in the society. The man would open one particular locker and drag a body out, leg first. It would be covered in a white sheet. The man would gently remove the cover from the face and move away to let Maa and Baba confirm identity. The man would then go ahead and give them a polythene containing my purse, my cellphone and a necklace Maa gave me a couple of years back. Maa would slowly walk towards the body. She would slowly touch the face and turn towards Baba.

"Dekho eta amader chotto tata" (Look, this is our little Tatai)

Baba would keep sobbing to himself, silently. Baba would gently hold Maa because I wouldn't be able to. I would never again, be able to. Maa would probably recite a line from Tagore, breaking down everyone's defences of being strong. Her reciting Tagore would be like a bullet to everyone's heart.

"Ache dukkho, aache mrityu" (there's grief and there's death), Maa would probably recite this particular song from Tagore. This was a song Tagore wrote after the death of Mrinalini Devi.

My death would be less effective a stimuli than her confirming it with a line from Tagore. My death would be more real when she would recall Tagore. Tears would keep rolling down her cheeks while she would caress my then cold face, devoid of emotions. I would never call her Maa again. I would never hug her again. I would never sing for her again. I would never sit beside her, trying to talk nonsense with her. I would never dig into her tummy with my head, claiming to go back into her womb as an adult again. I would never love her again. I would never share her happiness, her grief, her passions with her again. I would never go to beautiful horizons and exciting vistas with her again. I would never ask her to visit Delhi again and I would never ask her to bake for me again, or cook biryani for me again. Her life would break apart, as she would be fast forwarding through her memories and time spent with me, as she would look at my pale white face, cold to the touch. I was dead.

She would notice the huge wound to my head and would run her warm fingers on the wound. She would then, quickly and discreetly, medically examine it or whatever was left of it.

She would look at Baba and tell him what might have been the reason for death and probably what I experienced at the end.

"Khub koshto peyeche Tatai. Keu chesta o koreni amader chotto tatai ta ke bachanor. Porey chilo erom bhabei". (He must have been in so much pain when he died. No one even tried to save him. He bled out).

Catharsis with Maa

Baba would try to pull Maa away from me but she would keep coming back to my lifeless, dead, pale body claiming her rights over me. Baba would probably leave her with my lifeless, emotionless body while he would complete the legal formalities, ready to take me away to a burning ghat nearby. And while my body would be put into a hearse, adorned by garlands and flowers, Maa would hold my then stiff and slightly bulged hands. I would not be able to hold her hand back, because I would be dead but she would still keep holding my hands. She would look at my now closed and yet open eyes, eventually kissing them goodbye, one last time and then kiss my forehead and she would keep sobbing to herself. Every part of me, has memories etched in her brain. As she would run her eyes, down the man she created, she would keep sobbing to herself, trying to look away, without avail. As our relatives would help Baba carry my body into the furnace, Maa would not allow them to keep her away. She was too erudite a woman in a country like India. She was way too much educated for males asking her to stay away because she was a woman. She was too strong a woman to be held back. She was way too strong, a human to be held back But bringing me back to life was something, even she would never be able to do. She would silently hold one end of the wooden framework on which my body would be placed, making it ready to be burnt. The body would be placed on the metal rails which run into the furnace. The furnace door would open. Maa would break down into a fit of extreme grief sobbing to herself, one last time, in my dead presence. She would hug me the last time. Her tears would adorn my face the last time. She would run her fingers on my face and the vermillion from her forehead would be smudged on my face, the last time. And in the end, "Money re Aaj kohoje, Bhalo mondo jahai ashuk shotto re lawo shohoje" (Tell your mind, ready your mind and say it to yourself... Whatever may happen; whatever it is, however sad or however happy it is; accept it with ease), Maa would once again quote Tagore again, quoting his poem 'Bojhapora' this time around. Maa would look at me one last time before my body would be finally forwarded into the raging fire, where my flesh, my bones and my whole body would burn. She would never be able to spend time with me again. She would never touch me again. My body would be gone. She would never laugh with me again, nor would she play with my hair again. She would never look into my eyes, asking me about Tulika again. She would never see me running to hug her again or to tickle her ribs till she sat down. She would never have new memories of me trying to lick her ears, to irritate her. She would never have me as the first one to eat her overbaked cake. She would never have my company again. She would never sit behind me, on her scooty again and keep hitting my helmet with hers. She would never be able to wake me up in the morning for me to go out with her. I would not call her Maa again. She would never be a mother again.

And while she would break down into inconsolable fits of grief and cries she would at the same time, hug Tulika and cry it out, with her, sharing both their irreparable losses, realising that I'd never be a part of their lives again.

"Jokhon porbe na mor payer chinho ei bate" (one day we will be gone and out footsteps will no longer echo in these corridors, these paths- Tagore in the Magazine Probashi) Maa started to hum, while the ashes of my remains were brought out in a little container. Maa kept staring at the ashes as if like a phoenix, I would suddenly clamour to life once again, but as her eyes grew tired of crying and her voice choked from her tears suffocating her, she kept trying to mumble the song beneath all her grief. Maa picked up one piece of my bone and wrapped it in a handkerchief. She kept it in her bag.

"Tatai amar, abar ashbe" (my Tatai will come again).

Maa kept staring at the shackles we all wear, the prison of flesh and bone, now gone from my body. She looked at the ashes one last time before Baba eventually wiped his eyes, held hugged Maa and cried, for the last time in his entire life. He then slowly walked with the ashes to gloomy, smelly and guttery, squalored banks of the Yamuna river. He slowly emptied the entire remains of my ashes, finally freeing me from my corporal body into the elements which created me, long time back. Maa wept under her faint song till Baba came back and dragged her out of the inner sanctum.

She would probably faint a couple of times over the next few days. She would probably keep mumbling and reciting Tagore, Nazrul, Shankha Ghosh, Bankim and even Sukumar Ray[67]. No one would replace me for her,

---

[67] Tagore, Nazrul, Shankha Ghosh, Bankim, Sukumar Rayn were famous poets of Bengal in no particular order.

ever. Her endeavours in poetry, gardening, birdwatching would only try and take up more space in her life, with less effect but would keep her busy. In spite of Baba being there, my death; the loss of a child; a child she brought up with all the care and love in the world was like dying herself. But in the end, life would go on. She would engross herself in plants, even more, read even more, recite more Tagore, sing even more, cry at times and would get over my death. Well, not actually get over my death but she would learn to live with it. Baba would probably turn cold to every emotion by the time Maa would start making everyone smile again though.

For once I wish, I did die then, leaving Maa to survive me rather than me having to survive her absence. It's unnerving having to wake up, instinctually trying to reach for my phone, wanting to call her only to realise it was something I can never do again. It's equally dispiriting looking at a beautiful flower or bird only to realise Maa is not there to name it for me anymore. It's almost demoralising and tiring to go through her memories, playing them back one by one, trying to smile again, while she isn't there anymore. It's difficult, enduring and testing. For once I wish, it was me, not her! For once!

Day 21

Epistles which will never reach you

It's been three weeks, twenty one days since Maa is gone. Practically I've stayed months before I've met Maa in the past and empirically, it still feels like she's there, at home, waiting for me to return. It is almost as if, she as an entity still exists somewhere and I'm just somewhere else geographically, away from her. Me being at Gurgaon now just makes it easier to believe in that. Realistically, rationally she's somewhere I can't reach and probably, no, realistically I'll never reach again. She's on her finaly vacation, a vacation she'll never come back from. The pain of losing her, now, now lingers inside me, like a waning forest fire trying to grasp more trees. I keep trying to stay without having to think about Maa's absence but it's harder than I think it is.

Dear Maa,

I wish I could be in your arms again. I wish I could hear your voice again, stemming from your vocal cords, instead of this stupid phone which still has your recordings. I wish I could tell you how much I love you Maa and how much I wish to see you again. I wish I could grow old and see you grow older, age like fine wine eventually, while I would live my life out with all of you.

I wish I could take you to Norway, finally, and I wish we could see the Northern lights, together, while Baba would be happily smoking somewhere. I wish you could still make momos for me and I could still pester you to make me the best cakes I had in my entire life. I wish I could call you and discuss my entire day with you. I wish I could video call you, to see you tired and ask you to take care of yourself. I wish I could ask you to lower the volume on your phone and ridicule this habit of yours with Tua. I wish I could walk up to the terrace and find you there, watering the plants or silently doing something with some plants. I wish I could take you to all the plants nurseries in Kalyani, Jirat[68] and elsewhere and get you all the plants you want. I wish I could take you to Sattal once again and sleep right beside you, being able to hear you breathe and snore softly. I wish we could eat biryani together and talk about how ridiculous religion is. I wish I could get married while you would have tears in your eyes, glowing with pride to see your son happy with the love of his life, who loves you so much! I wish I could show you how happy I'm teaching my students and I wish I could give you their feedback. I wish we could complete our long awaited Ladakh trip in my car and I wish we could watch the stars together from a tent. I wish I could walk to the terrace at home and still find you reciting a poem while looking at a magnanimous sunset. I wish I could repair

---

[68] Kalyani is a city in Nadia district. The author's Maa used to visit this city to look for plants in the many orchards and nurseries here. Jirat is a city in the Hooghly district where the author's Maa also visited for the same reason.

your laptop, your phone and your gadgets. I wish I could drive you to your chamber again, where your patients would ask you why the driver looks so well-groomed and handsome! I wish to just sit with you and talk with you and discuss "Haw Jaw Baw Raw Law" (Sukumar Roy) with you. I wish I could tell you how less I get paid and how much more I aspire to earn. I wish to tell you how tired I am of people and how tired I am of smiling at everyone.

Dear Maa,

I wish you were here. I wish I could call you Maa again. I wish I could touch you again and feel the warmth of your touch again Maa. I wish you were here Maa. Dear Maa, I wish you were here!

Yours
Tata

Today when Maa isn't here anymore and I keep noticing flowers everywhere. I smell the fragrance of flowers and I silently shed tears in her memory. I find a beautiful sight and I cannot share it with anyone. I fail to understand why I had this abysmal misunderstanding that flora and fauna weren't that demanding of human attention and time. She was special, I've mentioned before. She had this special, subtle connection with nature, as if nature was hers and she was nature's. In the end, the woman who cried when a random tree was axed down and when thousands of trees broke down in the violent cyclone of Amphan and when the last tree in our house was broken down ages ago to accommodate a room, has been taken away by nature. She was too close to nature and nature has her now.

Arabicana Jasmine, the same flower which used to greet little me and Maa, every time we used to visit her paternal home, my Mamabari, is a common flower in India and now, in the age of plant nurseries and bustling commercial success of selling plants, it's everywhere because of its beautiful fragrance. Every time I am out walking or cycling, there are these places where I can smell the sweet smell of flowers including Jasmine. I am somehow teleported back to Maa's company. It suddenly feels like I am with Maa, little again, sitting behind her, riding pillion on her scooty, trying to hold her tummy, so that I don't fall down while Maa would keep explaining what flower it was. I would try and look behind her shoulders, so that I would be able to see what the flowers look like but I would terribly fail because I was little. Maa would inevitably stop the scooty and show me the flowers, helping me to identify them. When Boro Mama, Maa's elder brother passed away, Maa woke me up in the morning and softly told me that he was no more. I remember being taken to Mamabari that day, knowing I would never see him again. The flowers greeted us though. The flowers still had the sweet fragrance of spring summer, welcoming everyone in that inexpungeable grief. I was taken inside, where he was placed on a stretcher, now gone, once again, covered in a blanket of flowers, chandan on his face, garlands around his neck. While adults wept and sobbed, I just cried once and looked at Maa. Maa wiped my tears and said, "Tobuo

Shanti, tobu anondo, tobu ononto jaage"[69] (in spite of that, there's peace, there's happiness and there's the endlessness of eternity). When Maa was there, lying in a bed of flowers, now unemotional, unfeeling, unresponsive, inexpressive, insensitive, dispassionate, cold and indifferent I went into a flashback of all deaths that I've personally been hurt by leading to 22 March, when a part of me died with Maa. I remember trying to remove the garlands from her neck because I couldn't hold her head. I remember how light her head was, and the thin hair she had on her head. I remember the vermillion on her face and the deep cut marks on her neck due to the dialysis she went through the last day. Maa would have been alive, had it not been for some unfortunate incidents and I would right now, at 7.09am be getting ready for work, knowing that I would speak to Maa exactly around 8.30am. I grow colder, as days progress and I can feel lesser and lesser as Maa's death slowly moves away in time from the present. The pain doesn't go away though. It doesn't. The pain doesn't go away knowing that when I still look at pictures of her days before her death, she was so happy with Baba and Tua, happily travelling in Sandakfu, clicking pictures, playing with snow and hugging them. The pain doesn't go away knowing that she didn't want to die and she wasn't ready to die. The pain doesn't go away knowing that Maa could have been treated better and then she would be

---

[69] A line from Tagore's famous song Ache Dukkho Ache Mrityu. A line I think, best describes this book.

alive. The pain doesn't go away knowing that Maa saved thousands while thousands couldn't save her.

Now, I am terribly frightened of going back home. I cannot go back to the place Maa was at knowing I'll never see her again. I cannot go back home knowing I'll never be greeted by Maa, even again or knowing that I'll never hear her voice, ever again. I cannot go back home knowing that the biggest reason that was home was because Maa was there. I cannot go back home knowing that Baba will be there alone, sad, broken and would remind me terribly of Maa. I cannot go home knowing every inch of that place would bear witness to my time spent with Maa, every time we hugged, cried, laughed, sang, ate, walked, ran, looked at the sky and just slept in peace. I cannot going back knowing Maa doesn't exist anymore.

As I came back home today, Rambo, the beautiful beagle, followed me to my room today, in search for a room to sleep in. I let him. He quickly got up on the bed and lied down on the bed, with his body touching me. He slept in such a way such that a part of his body touched mine, so as to establish some sort of secure connection. What happened after that is pure bliss. As I kept caressing his furry coat, he slept, he snored and he kept sleeping in peace. He seemed like he had no care in the world. Whenever I would move, Rambo would get up suddenly to check if I'm still there and then when he would see he's still connected to me, he would sleep. Rambo reminds me of me, when I was very young. Just like many youths all over the world, I was also afraid of the dark, loud noises, people and anything which was not family. When no one could make me sleep, I would bury myself into Maa's arms and sleep, without a worry in the world. I would sleep as if being in her arms would be safer than the US presidential bunker and more calming and serene than the insides of a recording studio built with sound proofing in mind. The moment my eyes would open, Maa would just say,"Ghuma Ghuma" (sleep sleep) and like magic spoken, those two signifiers would suddenly do magic to my soul and I would go to sleep. Maa was a magician. There were so many things untold to Maa. I wish I could tell her so many things before she died.

Dear Maa,

I promise not to waste time and money over useless rituals when you die. I promise to donate your organs, that can be used to save someone. I promise to not make your death a big deal and suddenly push you into sainthood. I promise to keep on living my life, as soon as I can. I promise to eat good food and not stop eating because you are dead. I promise to be a good kid, even when I grow up. I promise to remember you and I promise to keep you in memory all my life. I promise to never wallow in my grief while life would pass me by. I promise to look up at the sky and wonder. I promise to go to new places and wander. I promise to try new experiences, meet new people and I promise to take care of Baba. He will smoke lesser, I promise. I promise to take care of Tua and our family. I can be no doctor but I'll try and feed them apples Maa, so that doctors can keep away. Kidding! I'll keep them safe. I promise to keep your plants safe and I promise to keep feeding the doves that came to you every morning as your early morning companions. I promise to sing, to write and to be happy. I promise to smile Maa. I promise to exercise and stay fit and I promise to consult a doctor, as soon as I feel a bit ill. I promise to not take things for granted and I promise to question anything which looks fishy. I promise to be the man you loved more than yourself and raised from a single cell to what I am today. I'll keep Tuli happy and I'll find time for family. I'll be good Maa. I'll take care of myself. I'll always love you Maa. You'll always be in my heart Maa.

Yours,
Tata

Everything is relative

*And we are just pawns
in the brief period of time we live in*

Time is a measurement of both duration and dimension. Time, unlike we imagine it to be is a different vector and relative. Mass slows down the space and time equation making time slower due to the gravitational time dilation, predicted by Einstein and now verified through experiments. Just like a body of immense mass and gravity, Maa attracted many people towards her and her being there slowed down time for them. I for a matter of fact have been privy to her presence for so long that I had almost forgotten that there will come a day when her presence would not be in existence anymore. I almost forgot how it feels like to spin alone in the cosmos without a star, a supermassive black hole, a galaxy or a universe to rotate around and call home. Last time I did that was when I first came to Delhi to study at JNU. I didn't expect that to come back to me again.

From the day she left us all to today, this morning, I've been imagining that Maa is still there, only to break down once in a while realising she's gone and then going into a temporary phase of cathartic relief, devoid of emotions post that. I don't need to imagine. Thirty one years with

Maa were enough to have given me enough experience about how Maa would do this and that. Everything I do in life would have a version in the past I would have done with her. What's even more surprising is that the moment I'm absent minded, I'm oblivious of the fact that Maa is gone.

What's hurts is when suddenly I'm taken back to the day I saw her last, the day I couldn't hug her, the day I couldn't speak to her, the day I couldn't hold her close, the day I couldn't kiss her warm forehead, the day she died.

This morning on my cycling stint, I was slower than usual. I had this ardent urge to look at every flower, smell the fragrance of a few as if to seek out their locations, went from pillar to post looking at the various kinds of trees I could see around me and the various birds which kept singing around them. I stopped multiple times to click pictures of Jacarandas, one little small yellow flower with a wasp in it, a white little flowers with spiders in them, one little thorny bush which looked scary and a couple of pigeons trying to parley about world peace. I came back home and I was going through the pictures when it happened. I suddenly realised I used to send these to Maa and now, I would not be able to, anymore. The one who taught me all these things, brought me into the world and brought me around to understand the beauty of flora and fauna is no more.

Such Moments suddenly make you question your existence or question the reality or query the simulation!

Catharsis with Maa

Such Moments are in plenty in my life now. Sending pictures to Maa would beget me replies with their names and probably with better pictures she has already clicked.

Be it the scaly breasted munia or the Asian paradise flycatcher, be it jacarandas or radhachuras[70], she would not fail to amaze me with her endless knowledge in flora and fauna. You ask the internet. I used to ask Maa. I knew her responses and solutions would be much more reliable. Now I've to rely on other sources for data, now that my mainframe is gone; now that Maa won't respond anymore. You ask Google. I used to ask her!

I used to ask her about everything I didn't know about or wanted to know about and she would give me answers to questions I'd ask and the narrate me stories about them. I used to share with her one problem and she would give me solutions to all my ailments and then tell me stories to accompany them. Now I'm left with stories, problems, ailments, flowers and petals, birds and birdcalls with no one to identify them. Now I'm left with pictures and videos with no one to share them with. Now I'm left with lonely mornings with no one to share them with. Now I'm left without Maa...

---

[70] Radhachuras – Peltophorum Pterocarpum – a beautiful flower found in Southern Asian countries. They are yellow in colour.

Memories

*I have this intense passionate desire
to go back to being young again*

I remember the day I cleared out Maa's shoulder bag in order for her things to be organised, one last time. It was a couple of days after the 22 of March. Everything I touched inside her bag had a different story to tell. I came across a white envelope. There were literally around 50 lozenges inside. Maa used to take such pouches while travelling. She loved eating lozenges and giving them to others when on a trip. Once in a while, she would open one lozenge per head and give them to everyone. I touched the lozenges and felt Maa in them. I remembered our last Sattal trip like it was yesterday. It was a long time back but I could almost feel Maa sitting right behind me, while I kept driving my car. She would hand out those lozenges and candies every thirty minutes. It was irritating and yet so adorable. She also had this habit of putting her leg behind my driving seat bulging the seat behind my lower back in the process. On being asked, she would immediately say, "No I didn't do it" with a funny smile. I still remember how happy she was when she caught the first sight of mountains and she started to sing. That was the last time I shared our for mountains with her, at the same time, while on a trip. I still can't get myself to believing the fact that I will never share such beautiful views with her again. Infant believe that Maa will never be there again, with tears in her eyes while looking at a scenic landscape or a salty sandy seashore or when watching birds in a sanctuary or when spotting orchids in a forest or when waiting for a tiger after an alarm call or when just simply sitting at the banks of Ganges, waiting for sunset. She will never come back. I will keep hearing her speaking to me. I will keep hearing her sing. She's gone, yet she's here, in all my memories.

I have this intense passionate desire to go back to being young again. Had the seven golden wishing orbs or the dragon balls[71] existed, I would wish on them just like Frieza[72] did or Goku[73] mistakenly did in dragon Ball GT. When I was young, I had less things to worry about. All I needed to think about was my school, my pencil box, my eating times, early to rise early to bed, prevention is the best cure, my television timings and the fact that it would

---

[71] Dragon balls – firstly, they are not what they sound like. They are 7 magical golden orbs, which when collected together give the collector one wish (on wish on Earth, 3 wishes on Namek and one mega-wish by collecting the Super Dragon Balls)

[72] Frieza – a villain from the anime and manga series, Dragon Ball by Akira Toriyama.

[73] Goku – the protagonist of the anime and manga series, Dragon Ball by Akira Toriyama

or would not clash with anyone else's time, going out with my cycle, going out to the central grounds in Chinsurah to play cricket (at least miserably failing at fielding), going to tuitions, completing homework, not having to be eyewitness to Maa and Baba fighting or in turn stopping them, getting one rupee coins from Amma for Phuchka (gol gappe), eating Kul bhaja (fried red date or Indian date) with masala outside school, getting to visit video parlours with Baba and Maa and finding out video tapes of films we would watch on Baba's Video cassette player and not having to write something like this.

The existence of Maa was in plenty and I never imagined I would have to live without her, ever. When I was young, I cried but it was because I didn't get to watch the cartoon or anime I wanted to watch and Amma was busy watching some stupid Bengali soap.

When I was young I cried because Maa would probably slap me straight and square on my face because I scored low in the exams and hid the answer paper from Maa. I cried because Maa didn't agree to take me to watch Stuart Little and then later took me to watch it because I cried.

I cried because I saw Maa cry. I cried so many times because she was sad about something. She would just hold me and cry. I didn't know why she was crying but I would just hold her and cry. Maa wasn't able to cry, telling me how much she was in pain, the last time, because I wasn't there. Now I don't worry about television timings.

Now I don't play cricket. Now I don't go out to meet friends. I keep crying alone. Maa will never come and stop me now or take me in her arms, calming me. Now I've grown up, there are so many things to worry about and so less time. Now I cry, but alone and when no one is looking. I wish I was young again. I wish I could go back to when Maa would still be scolding me and the biggest of my worries would my parents not getting called to the school. There goes my childhood.

Every human has this stupid list we call the bucket list. Maa had one too. Maa wanted to travel more. Maa wanted to visit beautiful green forests on mountains, near the sea, near meadows of green and blue and near deserts and semi-arid places.

Maa wanted to see the Northern lights in person, the beautiful aurora borealis. Maa wanted to see me marry the love of my life, Tulika. Maa wanted to just sit, be at ease and rest. A couple of months back Maa told me, "Tatai retirement er por tor baba ar ami shudhu ghurbo. Tora time pele amader shaathe jabi" (After we retire, we will travel the world. When you can make time, join us).

Maa wanted to travel, learn, empathize and be at so many places. Life had different plans for her though. Life probably didn't want her to remain in this God forsaken hopeless planet, increasing its harsh conditions every day from fossil fuels to the Sahara increasing in size; from more unsustainable sources of energy to blatant pollution.

Maa didn't have to live long enough to wear a gas mask in a polluted apocalyptic world. Maa didn't live long enough to hear names of disorders and diseases like 'mobile addiction syndrome' or 'thumb-o-mobilitis' or 'her-mobile-pes' or something like 'numb brain'. Maa didn't live long enough to see nations torn apart by divisive governments. Maa didn't live long enough to see climate change convert her home into a barren heath. Maa lived long enough to see greens and blues, life and happiness.

Why I Hate Birthdays and Spring!

And why they make me sad

I don't like celebrating my birthdays. I've always believed that mothers should be celebrated. I haven't done anything while Maa has carried me for nine months bearing all pains, my kicks, planning our future together and she's lived carefully so that she can deliver a perfectly healthy me. It's like celebrating the fact that you've landed a great job and forgetting the years of toil before that. It's like forgetting that NASA, ISRO and other similar concerns have been trying endlessly to explore space and then celebrating one day, humankind's first mission to Pluto; forgetting that we are still prepping for it. Why do we celebrate birthdays? Commercialisation? Just so that on a particular day a person spends more than they would or because people around them can make them feel special on a particular day, gift them some more happiness, make them forget all pains? Probably! Everybody forgets their mother when it's their birthdays and hang out with their friends, booze, party and come back home, only to find out that their mother and father are still waiting for ten minutes of their time. It's sad how we claim to love them and yet in all fairness forget to make them a part of our lives. My life was pretty different. Maa was mostly there in most of my birthdays when I celebrated them. I would make it a point to celebrate it with Maa. I generally hate celebrating my birthdays and probably this year and in years to come it would be no different. Maa won't be there to wish me, hug me and fluff my hair kissing my forehead. The woman who made me who I'm; the woman who made me is gone. How do you think I can celebrate in spite of that?

It's spring and there's a plethora of colours I can see around me when I go out. Maa would have loved it. I'm growing this apathy towards everything, every day that I grow distant from Maa's touch. I've this innate hatred towards socialising, talking or even speaking at all, with anyone. I have this desire to just sit in a corner and be forgotten. Maa would have loved these play of colours in the environment now. Maa would have loved the lilac in Jacarandas, the red in Krishnachuras[74], the red orange pink and chrome in Bougainville, the red and pink in roses, the white and off white in arabicana Jasmine and the orange and yellow in marigolds. Maa would have loved it all. These colours cause me pain now; pain owing to the fact that Maa will never discuss these again. Maa will never see these colours again and I will never get to hear her beautiful expressions and emotions be emoted, ever again!

---

[74] Krishnachura – Delonix Regia – a beautiful flower found in Southern Asian countries. Trees with this flower make it look like the tree is on fire from a distance

A Series of Unfortunate Events

That led to
what should not have happened

It all started on the third day when they were all in Sandakfu. Maa felt extremely tired and drowsy. Maa wanted them to go along while she would rest for the day. Her hands were cold but she didn't realise it was something else. It was already cold and that masked the lack of peripheral circulation in her body. Maa slept while they toured around the area. Baba remembers Maa suddenly hallucinating at night and waking up to realise she was hallucinating. The next morning she was taken to a hospital in Darjeeling where she was given fresh high flow oxygen. She revived partially and the doctor advised her to be taken to a super speciality hospital. That's when she was taken where the final nail in her coffin was hammered. It was there, where due to the apparent apathy, lack of experience and incompetence that Maa's health deteriorated. She went into Uremia[75], her liver and

---

[75] Uremia – A medical condition when the blood in a person's body contains highly elevated levels of uric acid and creatinine

kidneys almost stopped working and yet, she was allowed to be transferred to Kolkata, being told that she was absolutely stable. Baba and Kaku didn't know this was going to happen. They were extremely confident when I kept calling them about Maa's whereabouts. Little did they know that they were being misled by this assuring doctor in Siliguri. Little did they know that the very next morning, Maa, then in pain but under no life support, would go from no life support, to ventilation to being inside a glass box, filled with flowers, being cried over by thousands and I would be in a corner trying to get a glimpse of her while she would leave our home for the last time, never to come back again. Little did they know that in a time period of less than twelve hundred minutes, she would go from stable to unstable to a bunch of flesh and bones, devoid of any memory of the last sixty years she has lived on earth. Little did they know I would never see Maa again when they spoke to me on the night of 21 March. Little did they know she would die. Little did they know, that Maa would not make it home, ever again and that she would lose conscience for the last time, with her eyes fixated at her love, Baba, while he desperately tried to do everything to make Maa survive. Little did they know that Maa's last words would be those which came from a doctor even in such pain, " Intubate me. I'm in acute respiratory stress". Little did they know that she was going through a condition known as thrombosis in pulmonary embolism. It was on the way back to Kolkata

---

respectively, leading to delusions, nausea, drowsiness and in extreme cases, death.

Catharsis with Maa

that she suddenly collapsed after saying her last words. They rushed her to the nearest ICU enables hospital which was only metres away, luckily. As they rushed Maa into the hospital with Baba and everyone else busy trying to hasten up things, Maa kept staring at the walls of the hospital as she was being rushed into it, slowly feeling her world fade around her; slowly feeling the colours desaturate; slowly feeling herself fall into a dark abyss of unconsciousness, a realm she didn't know she will never recover from. She went unconscious and the doctors tried everything to revive her. They say that she responded to the cardiac fibrillators the first time but the second time her heart went into shock, nothing helped. She was gone. Baba was outside trying to pay money and fill the forms when the doctor came out and told him what happened. Maa was gone; gone while I was busy trying to make it inside Delhi airport; gone while everyone was sleeping early morning at 4.50 am. Maa was released from her corporal body leaving us all to inherit her 'will of fire'[76]. Maa was gone.

---

[76] Will of fire – a concept propounded in the anime and manga Naruto, by Masashi Kishimoto. Asura Otsutsuki, the propounder of this idea believed that love is the main ingredient for peace.

Fur One More Time!

Once upon a time in a family from a faraway galaxy on a string vibrating to a different frequency

There's very less time before I die...

The stillness in her eyes took away all the life I thought I would have of living with her. I called her and she didn't look at me. She didn't know me anymore. I wish, for once, that she would suddenly remember who I was and then look into my eyes, once again, the way she used to; but maybe she never will. Taking her in my arms while she would bite my ears and play with tufts of my hair would never happen, again; ever again. She would never walk again. She would never smile again. She won't ever look at me, be lively and happy and come into my arms, ever again. She won't kiss my cheeks. She never will, again. Sometimes, life is unfair. Years of frozen tears in the heart, came back to me in a moment of catharsis.

The last time I was this broken was when she, Alice, had to go, and a part of me was deleted forever; gone. It's difficult but sometimes you have to kill the person you are. Your habits and your personality have been embedded in relationships, polished through every interaction that you have had and blended with what we call as social behaviour. They make you who you are. That was six years back. All that remains of her now, are pictures, videos and fond memories, a lot of them!

She was still. She was breathing because she had to. There was an emptiness in her eyes I can't define. Hazy, is what I would call her and my eyes. I just could not get through to her. Tears kept rolling down my cheeks as I wished she didn't have to go away.

Shifting to a new place immediately after she was gone, made it easier for me to get used to the new life. New faces, new roads, new places and new voices made me feel like I had outgrown the pains and blemishes of the last life. Unfortunately, she would linger on in my memories and I would reflect over every moment I had spent with her while I closed my eyes but slowly and steadily I got over the fact that she was no longer with me and that those 12 years of bliss would just be a ghost of the beautiful past.

I used to go back home every six months or so, to meet the ones who still love me more than I ever loved them, my parents. They know, that its only for them I went back. And when I went back home a few months back, I saw her for the first time. She was beautiful, she was small and she was too cute to be real. She was plump and she looked innocently into my eyes as I approached her. She couldn't move. She was too young. She could not even chew the biscuit I gave to her. I picked her up as she kept wagging her extremely small tail, peeing on my hands entirely. She would be extremely elated to see me. She would keep waiting for the pieces of biscuits I would give to her and the sweets she would get from me, to eat. Something was not right. Any time the world seems like it is perfect is when things go haywire. When you are extremely happy is when you are facing the maximum chances of losing everything.

Somehow something was forcing me to be apathetic to a stray puppy, who I knew was cute, but had nothing to do with me. She had this wonderful energetic charm which made me fall prey to her. We formed a bond; a bond stronger than most humans would ever make. She and I shared so many beautiful Moments. But I had to leave home and come back and knew she would grow up in leaps and bounds, as the seasons passed.

I was anxious and I wanted to meet her. I wanted her to recognize me. I wanted her and me to share the same bond we had months back. Maa told me that she had grown up to be a strong lady. She surprised me. She jumped up into my arms, bit my hair and licked my ears. Nothing had changed; nothing at all. I could discern the surprise on my Maa's face. She said she never seen her this energetic in weeks. It seemed as if she was reciprocating what I felt for her; the little beautiful ball of fur. And sailed, thereafter, the boat of happiness. Playing with her all day and taking pictures, jumping along, running along the lawns and lying down on the cold floors while she would sneak her furry warm head on my lap and then suddenly being licked on the cheeks, went on in repeat. She would become a lost soul, if I would not be at home.

A part of me identifies deeply with the soul of a dog. The level of loyalty and friendship I have experienced from the other side of my life 6 years back, with Alice; losing it thereafter; and then this young lady teaching me once again, to love them back, the way they deserved to be loved, made me feel excited; very excited. There was this energy in me that being in her presence would awaken. Six years back, I buried all warm feelings for these furry heads, in general along with Her, but somehow they kept coming back to me in all shapes and sizes. I was relieved that I would never fall in love with them again; never entrust my happiness to them again…but life has surprizes for you; always!

A sudden dark cloud descended on the valley of beautiful flowers. A blotch of black was suddenly painted onto a canvas of white. A perfectly functioning mechanism, a perfectly functioning technicality stopped working. Poor life!

Two weeks back she stopped eating. She started to cough. She started to lose control. She had terrible muscle convulsions and she was afraid. She forced herself into a corner. I was afraid of the worst but I immediately arranged for medicines and medical aid. She started to heal but she was weak. I stayed right beside her. I watched her as she slept. I ran my fingers through her fur as she slept and she kept breathing, in pain and in peace. Events and memories from six years back, before She left us all, came back to me. I was afraid. I was haunted by old memories.

A few mornings passed. She was still lying down. The medicines made her sleepy. I wanted her to look at me, play with me and sleep in my lap. She didn't respond to me. I called her again and she did not respond again. I showed her a biscuit and she bit the biscuit, along with my finger. In her present condition, she was, at best, what I would say, mostly vegetative. She had succumbed to her brain injuries, as a result of the convulsions. She had a beautiful temperament but distemper got the best of her. She didn't know who I was. She refused her favourite foods and was afraid of me. She did not want to play with me. She did not want me to pat her coat of beautiful white and black fur. She did not want me!

A few mornings went by and she could not smell or see things given to her. As Moments passed, I waited in extreme fear, for the moment I feared the most. Perhaps the only consolation I had for myself was that she was not in pain, or perhaps she was. Once, just once, I wished that she could speak again, play with me again. I wish she would speak to me and tell me what she was feeling. She was just a baby, not even a year old. She closed her eyes one last time. I wished for her to look at me again and wag her tail. She did not. I wish, she would jump into my arms once again and bite my hair. She did not.

She lied down lifelessly, just like the first time I met her. Life is such a cycle! Her life came full circle, too soon. Life seemed to have gone back to the moment I had met her. A poignant music played as I kept looking at her, as she breathed in pain. I did not know if an afterlife existed and still do not do but if it did and does, I would have surely wanted to meet her once again and be in her company. Frozen tears and pent up emotions all came back to me. It had been six years since I had buried Her, buried Alice, and united her with the soil. It all kept coming back to me. I was not ready. I was not ready to die, once again.

Happiness, friendship, loyalty, love, companionship and togetherness, everything came to me from these four legged furry souls. They have given me a lot more than I ever did to them. We don't understand them. We do not listen. They want to talk. They want to emote. They always do. Even while she was lying down lifeless, she wanted me to realize and appreciate, so many beautiful things we shared in the last few months. She wanted me to realize she loved me a lot and that even if I could not make time for her while she was growing up, she had never forgotten me. She wanted me to realize that life goes on, and that in spite of losing people closest to us, we must move on and not break down.

A poignant music played as I close my eyes, playing back all the memories of sunlit days, moon-kissed nights, cloud caressed and lowly lighted Moments I had spent with her. The music kept playing as the numbered hours, disappeared into the dark slowly and gradually.

She breathed in pain, while I waited to die, once again!

~~His~~ Her- Story

Breaking stereotypes, gender roles and unneeded traditions, one signified at a time

I remember watching the films 'Baby's day out, 'Jurassic Park, 'Flubber', 'Sonar Kella', 'Extra Terrestrial', 'Gupi Bagha' and many other classics with Maa at the theatres. On the other hand, I also remember watching 'Chaad-er-pahar' a Bangla film with her at a local theatre, a film through which I mostly slept. I remember going to watch it because Maa was going alone. I remember how much she appreciated me sitting (sleeping) through the bring film with horrific VFX. It damaged me for life but her company probably saved me from that horror. It won't anymore.

I remember going to boring talk shows with her, accompanying her to medical conferences, eating at places with her and all with her. I thought we were inseparable. It didn't occur to me that Maa would die someday. It didn't occur to me that as we were slowly and steadily creating memories together, we were also making us vulnerable to a greater fall. Slowly and steadily, as we grew closer, the chances of us losing more parts of us, when either of us would die, were increasing. But the human mind does not think that way! We entrust our emotions in each other, invest our lives in each other; and she was a mother. She did that unconditionally; never turned back; never regretted it.

Tua has this extreme lack of balance break and coordination when it gets to riding a cycle or even while walking. Maa always wanted her to lead on her legacy of riding the scooty. When Maa started to ride her scooty, she was one of the two lady riders in town and it was the talk of town. A woman, who was also a doctor, was riding her own scooty, not being chauffeured by her husband; going everywhere on her own, breaking stereotypes, gender roles and unneeded traditions, one signified at a time. Incidentally the other lady who rode another scooty in the town at that time, was another doctor and eluded the same magnificence! She lives though. Time went by and 28 years later, there are thousands now. Tua still has to learn riding the scooty. Coincidentally, a couple of days back she called me early morning.

"Dada, guess where I am"

"Next to your phone?"

"No no. Be serious"

"Where are you? The bigger question is how are you up so early?"

"I am out with Baba. I rode his scooty, with him riding pillion and I did it right."

"Whaaaat?! I wish Maa could see it."

There was this awkward pause for a few seconds.

"Maa wanted you to ride her scooty."

"Yes dada, I will now. I can be her legacy now"

And that's how our conversation ended; poignant yet happy.

The Paradise

That became a civilized mess

We had six feet of garden around our home from the early memories of home I had. It was adorned by beautiful trees and flowers and I remember being privy to smelling new smells, new fragrances every day. One afternoon Dadu decided to construct a new guest room. It required a massive part of that perimeter six feet garden to be sacrificed. Dadu got it built because Maa needed a private chamber of sorts at home as well. I remember my earliest memories of picking up soil and playing with plants, recognising plants. I remember picking up flowers and trying to mix them in a bowl to make colour our of them. I remember trying to cook by fake cooking twigs and leaves and trying to feed that to my Amma. I remember chewing on random leaves and sucking the honey out of flowers. I remember writing the first letters I learnt using written scripts of language in the garden soil. I remember falling down, getting up and I remember growing up for quite some time, in there. I remember the cyclone of 1993 and how the walls of Gorosthan[77], the Dutch cemetery broke after it. I remember it all.

Maa came back home from the hospital drenched in rain a couple of times and she complained how when she started off it was dry but by the time she was half way the sky turned dark grey and started raining only Moments before she reached home. She would be so pissed. In spite of being what she called 'bhijey chuppush' or 'bhijey toitumbur' or 'bhijey roshogolla' (all meaning drenched), she would then fetch chappatis from the morning and feed the four legged furry friends of ours. They, also drenched, would still come to eat. But this didn't happen now. It's been some time since I've been dreaming about Maa now. I dreamt about this in the morning today. My eyes opened soon after and I realised she was gone. I felt so empty, lonely and desperate for her touch. Nothing in the world can give me what I want. Nothing will bring me Maa.

Driving lessons were difficult with Maa. She had a will of steel but her age and reflex didn't allow for her skills to grow. She was slow at best, when it came to learning to drive but she wanted to learn it. I was teaching her to drive and yet she was the one still teaching me, inspiring me, indirectly informing me that even at old age, one can be self-sufficient, interdependent yet independent. I'm happy she drove my car though. She sat in that seat, I sit in

---

[77] Gorosthan – a Bangla word for a graveyard and the local name for the Dutch Cemetery in Chinsurah; an enormous cemetery located next to the author's home.

everyday to drive. She drove my car. And even if she would stop the car the moment she would see a truck coming from the opposite lane, from far away and let it pass, she still did drive. I wish I could go back to those days when I would be able to shout at her in frustration, prompting her to get pissed with me, meaning I would try to get her to calm down again and hug her in the end. I wish Maa was here, again.

She Was Crying Absolutely Helplessly

When I walked in...

I remember how helplessly Tulika was crying, sitting just next to Maa. I remember how they first started off on the wrong foot and how by the end, they were inseparable. It took me a year of talking to Maa and hours of trying to make her understand that Tulika and I were really serious about each other and it wouldn't end up being a fling. It took me so much time to explain to Tulika that my Maa is a bundle of nerves and she loves me dearly. She would never ever hand me over to someone else. She would want to keep her only son, hers.

Tulika was scared at first but soon, Maa started liking Tulika. By the end of the second year, they met each other a lot, while I was here wondering what they were eating. The day Maa asked me about when we would get married was only a year back. How did it get to now?! Maa planned everything for us, with great care, in great details. Tuli and Maa shared a bond which goes far beyond mother in law and daughter in law definitions and signifieds.

Seeing Tulika cry like that took me back eight years back, when we first started dating, when Maa was alive and made me wish we were suddenly back in 2013 when Maa was alive and I didn't have to cry alone. It took me back to 2013 when I could touch Maa, listen to her voice, be with her and hug her.

Richard Dawkins[78], as read in "Letters from an Astrophysicist" by Neil deGrasse Tyson has been an amazing read. A few things have given me perspective.

The ones who can die are the lucky ones. Genetic combinations of who could never exist, will never be born, never live their life and never die. Amongst the trillions of combinations the human genome sequence can regurgitate, there are many which never come to being. There are many which never take birth! Only a handful take birth.

Only a handful survive the post-natal critical period and then finally only a handful get to live out their lives, experience everything and then finally face death. Death is beautiful when you consider the fact that it comes to only those who get to live life. It's beautiful when you consider that only the lucky ones get to live!

---

[78] Richard Dawkins – A biologist and scientist; most popular for his theories on how gene as the principle factor in selection for evolution

Trillions of microorganisms once living off the human body, die with the human body ending metabolism for the last time and as the human body cools down from its 98 degree Fahrenheit temperature, it slowly cools to the touch.

The microbes have a gala feast for the last time and then either become refugees or try and transfer over. When the body is cremated, most of these harmless, helpful microbes die with the body.

I guess I would love to be buried when I die. Like Neil deGrasse Tyson[79] says, I would also love to be buried when I die.

It's true that I wouldn't know what would happen but let this book be a testament to my will. In being buried, I'd not useless commit genocide on huge colonies of bacteria and in the process I'd add on as food to nature (I've taken a lot from nature and will keep taking, till I die. The least I can do is give back)

---

[79] Neil deGrasse Tyson – an astrophysicist, scientist, philosopher and empiricist; one who holds an enormous effect and inspiration for the author.

The Curious Case of the Bucketing Meniscus

When the meniscus in my knee decided to take a vacation

In the year 2018, I met with an accident and my left knee meniscus was torn. I had a bucket handle tear and I couldn't open my knees in months. I couldn't walk for almost one and a half months. I thought I would never walk again. Maa and Baba didn't come to Delhi then because I didn't let them know how grave the situation was. By the time they came to know, Didi was already getting me treated. I remember Maa's soothing voice and how she tried to soothe me. I remember how Maa spoke to multiple doctors, discourses held, and how she came to her conclusions, no matter what they were, giving me hope. Maa always gave me hope. Had it not been for Maa and Tulika's follow up, I would probably still be crippled now... Maa! Where are you when I need you to fix me now? I remember this conversation with both Maa and Tulika. They both had very similar responses.

"Maa what if I can never walk again?"

"You will walk again! This is temporary. Science begets future telling through empirical reasoning. I tell you you will be fine, because I have proper empirical reasoning to tell you so. Stop whining. Face the pain now. You will be fine in a couple of weeks. "

"I am just afraid Maa. You sure, I will be fine?"

"Yes. Keep taking the meds and keep doing the exercises"

"Maa can I come home? I want to be with you both. I feel lonely here, now that I cannot walk"

"You cannot walk now. Coming back home would be a logistics nightmare if you cannot walk. Give your knee two weeks and then book a ticket home. By then you will be able to walk with your walking stick, without completely needing to rely on it." I remember how cocooned I felt and even if I had extreme pain in the left knee. I had this urge to continue physiotherapy every day, instead of wallowing in my shell of hopelessness because I would finally be home, with them. Maa gave me the will to smile, in the face of adversities and yet, ironically when she is gone, she is not here to help me smile, once again! Maa wasn't here when I finally underwent the meniscus repair surgery in May 2022 and then had to go through two months of intensive frustration training, when I first could not walk, then could not walk properly, then could not bear the pain from walking and then suddenly realise that Maa was not here with me to comfort me. Maa wasn't here to comfort me because barely a few months back she left us all. Everyone else was here with me. Everyone else came to see me. Maa didn't.

◆

Childhood

From the earliest on memories I have

Maa used to take me to her place of work when I was very young. I remember Maa sitting at her chair in the outdoor patient unit and talking to thousands of patients. I remember their reverence for Maa and I remember how obedient they were to Maa's comments and prescriptions. I remember the smell of medicine all around me and how in spite of that, I fell in love with the world of medicine.

I guess this was when I started aspire to become a doctor like Maa but eventually as I grew up I became a doctor of philosophy! When I grew up, I never went inside her chambers; obviously; but I always went to receive her. That won't ever happen again. I'll never enter that hospital ever again! Maa won't be there and that building would be the remnant of a once majestic and royal time period Maa spent there.

From the earliest on memories I have, I remember how we are trained about what we need to know and not how to think. This cripples us as thoughtful individuals.

I've been thinking how humans have created the system of society, entailing details of birth and death, happiness and sadness, famine and plenty. We are taught that the sun sets and sun rises instead of being told that the rotation of the earth sends the sun at an angle which is beyond that of the curvature of the earth from certain portions, making it feel like the sun is actually going down. I fail to comprehend how in the grand scheme of things, in spite of me being taught the right way by Maa to be rational and empirical, to be inductive rather than deductive, to be epistemologically sound, I end up imagining Maa to be alive.

I question what caused her to die and I keep pondering on which of those thousands of decisions that she took, was wrong, going back and changing which, would assure her existence today. I guess I'm still in denial after twenty eight days of her being gone. Time flies! It's been twenty eight days since I saw Maa last and yet I cannot shrug off the feeling that she's here, with me. However, empirically she's gone! No matter how much I rationalize, I end up crying to myself, desperately trying to hold her again, talk to her again, kiss her again and make her come back; again.

The earliest memories after birth I have are of Maa feeding me milk from a bowl while I would busily try and barf it out. I remember Baba seating me in front of the bike to go get Maa from the hospital she was posted at. I remember biting Maa on her chin at the terrace for some reason and her crying afterwards because I bit hard. I remember patiently waiting for Maa while playing with various toys downstairs in the TV room and I remember being happy when Maa returned home and hugged me.

I remember her taking me to various places with me standing in front of her scooty, on the footboard, without a helmet, because no one knew what one was until ten years later. I have 'n' number of memories with her.

Sometimes you don't know the value of a moment, until it becomes a memory.

Day 30

Exactly one month after her demise

It's exactly one month since I was in that flight back to Kolkata. Maa was in a state of constant flux. She was Schrodinger's[80] cat. It was only at 9.10am, exactly 30 mins from now that, she died for me, even if her actual death occurred way before, around 4.50am. I have been steadily yet dreadfully trying to bridge the gap between expectations and knowledge. I've been trying to bridge the gap between what I subconsciously expect with what the truth is. Everyday has been difficult and yet a breeze of fresh air. There has been Moments when I absolutely broke down and lost all sanity. There haa been Moments when I just stood with my head to the wall, crying till I felt my toes feel my teardrops and yet, there has been

---

[80] Erwin Schrodinger – won the Nobel prize for physics in 1933 by founding the study of wave mechanics. In a thought experiment the scientist ponders how a cat is both alive and dead, when locked in an opaque box. Until the cat has been taken out of the box, no one knows if the cat is dead or alive. The moment the cat has is taken out is the moment we finally get closure on the condition of the cat. When the cat is in the box, the cat is both dead and alive at the same time.

Moments when I've, yet, smiled again. Even today my body and mind struggles to retain the fact that Maa is gone. Even today I've to consciously remind myself that it's over! Even today in some other, beautiful reality, Maa is alive and with me! Here, in this universe; not so much!

It's ironic how exactly one month after her demise, I'm here, sitting with a runny nose and a sore throat without Maa there to advise me on medicines. My doctor is dead. She is gone.

It's ironic how I'm stuck in a situation where I feel helpless and there's no help. I don't feel as invincible anymore. I don't feel as invincible as Maa made me feel when after 2 months of prolonged pain in the knee, I learnt to walk again; ran again. I don't feel invincible. Today I can walk, run, trek, feel the warm ground beneath my feet and yet a simple cold makes me feel endangered. Maa isn't there to cure me.

It's ironic how, exactly at the time when she died, in the morning at 4.50am, I woke up with eyes wide open, tears rolling down my cheeks. It's ironic how the world has lived on, while she didn't.

It's ironic that I'll get married while she's gone. She won't be there to see me get married to Tulika and she won't be there to bless us (no matter how irrational that is since human beings cannot change the course of time).

It's ironic that in this cosmos there are no accidents (every incident has a reason for happening and everything happens because it has an event which foreruns it.

Nothing is an accident. There is no magic. Eventually everything can be explained. That which is unexplainable now, is what we call magic. Knowledge of the subject would change magic into science. That which is magic somewhere, is science elsewhere!) and yet she died before the average death age for females in the country.

It's ironic that she was a doctor who saved thousands, if not millions and yet doctors could not save her.

It's ironic that patients continue to call her phone number and ask for help from her, only to get to know that she is dead and now they need to look for another doctor! It's ironic that the world is moving on. I have been trying to hold on to all her memories, trying not to forget even one. Forgetting her memories make me feel like she's dying, all over again.

One month back, when she was in that glass covering, in the hearse, I wanted to believe that it was a joke and that she would wake up again. I wanted to believe that Maa would suddenly shrug all the flowers aside, wake up and criticize everyone who has killed so many beautiful flowers and then in the end declare that it was all, a joke! I wanted to believe that Maa would wake up, shrug aside the cover of death, that enveloped her being. I wanted to believe that she wasn't leaving her home, for the last time. But alas! She was! And as people flocked around me, some wailing, some crying, some commenting on how her time had not yet come and yet some simply touching her feet as if she was a deity, I simple stood there, stupidly looking at her. I stood there belonging to her. I stood there, teary eyed, trying to make sense of what was happening.

Catharsis with Maa

I stood there as the rituals of parting went ahead. In the end the cage was about to close and she would then be taken to a blast furnace, to be seen no more! Before they closed the gates, I gently held her two feet but I didn't treat her like a deity. Maa taught me to be empirical and rational at the same time. She taught me to be reasonable and logical. I kissed her feet gently. I loved her a lot and I just wanted to kiss her, goodbye. Loved, in past tense because the moment she died, our relation ended. I ended being a son for my mother. I ended receiving love from her. I stopped being a son for a mother, altogether. Loved, in past tense, because Maa was gone and I stood there, as the glass cage closed. Maa was in the process of receiving freedom from her prison of blood and bone[81] and yet remain caged in that little glass prison. I stood there as the car slowly started moving, signalling her last goodbye. I stood there looking as Maa left her home for the last time...

---

[81] A concept propounded by Rabindranath Tagore. We die and get freedom from our body; a prison of blood, flesh and bone.

Too Little Too Soon

Little did I know that I would never see
her again, in person

20 February and I was about to leave home again. I wanted to meet Maa before I left for Gurgaon, back to work. That time, I went back home for the wedding of a friend of mine and stayed home for a couple of days. It was around 12.30 pm and I had to leave by 1.30pm in order for me to reach on time, at the airport, in time to board the flight to Delhi. I called her around 1 pm and she said she was on the way back home.

I was downstairs as she entered the garage, with her familiar stance, tiptoeing with her scooty and then parking it inside. She quickly entered the dining room and sat down with me to have lunch, while I was eating with Tua and Baba. I asked Maa if she was free post lunch and if she would accompany me to the airport, to drop me there. Maa, a doctor, was a very busy person but she found time for me; lot of time. She accompanied me that day.

Tua sat in the front seat and I was with Maa, in the backseat. It is around 60 kilometres from our place to the Dum Dum airport and it took us around one hour and twenty five minutes; the last one hour twenty five minutes I had spent with Maa; a fact I did not know at that time.

As the car sped through familiar roads and the rustic countryside of Bengal being slowly overtaken by civilized promoted property, I gently put my head on her shoulders and tried to close my eyes for a quick sleep. She put her hands on my head and patted my head. I hugged her and closed my eyes but I could not sleep. The car was shaking and all I could think about was the fact that I would not see Maa, Tua, Baba, Tulika, my family and the place I grew up in, for a long time. As time ran out, I put my head in her lap.

"Erom bacchader moton shuye porli? (You had to sleep like a baby? Really?)"

"Kano go? Problem ki? (Why? What is the problem?)"

And with that conversation done, I stayed there, in her lap for another twenty minutes. And as I closed my eyes, all I felt was pain; the pain of separation. I had this deep connection with Maa and I always tried not to cry in front of her because she was so empathetic, she would cry. I kept flashing back to all the memories I had spent at home. I kept thinking about my decision to leave my job at Kolkata and come back to Gurgaon and I kept wanting to stay with them, my parents, with Maa and Baba. I could not. And, as all of this was happening, I slowly held Maa's hand.

We reached the airport and as I stepped out of the car, I felt sad. I felt sad, because I was going back. I was sad because I was not social and no one broke into my inner sphere like Maa and my family and because I might smile at everyone but I rarely share or socialize well! I felt sad because I would miss spending time with Maa, the most.

I still go back to memories of that day. That was the last photograph I clicked with her, a selfie. She was sad and yet happy to have been with me. I was trying to stop my flood gates and Tua, just like always, was the heart of the picture, bringing in happiness, frivolity and life into the picture. That was the last picture. That was the last time I shared pieces of scattered happiness with her. That was the last time I felt her holding me in her arms, kissing my forehead. That was the last time I felt maternal care! That was the last time we shared our mutual issue of not emoting that we were sad at my departure to Delhi and yet, with our para-lingual communication, we knew, we were sad. That was when I expected to meet her in May, in a couple of days from now. That was when I knew I would see her again, on our next trip to Sattal. It has always been like this. There were rare occasions when Maa would cry and vocally hug me while I left. She mostly did not emote, like I don't. Most of our memories have us just hugging each other, talking with our eyes and going our different ways, when I came back to Delhi.

Little did I know that I would never see her again, in person. I would have frozen time at that instant, stayed with her and held her with all my strength. I would never let her go. Little did I know that those twelve hundred seconds were the last twelve hundred seconds I spent with the woman I loved the most. Little did I know that when I would see her the next time, I would see her lifeless, cold and dead, covered in a heap of flowers, not being able to sad at the death of so many flowers or be happy at the fact that I was there, right by her side. Little did I know, she had exactly thirty days to live. It was too little, too soon!

I have made a cocoon for me there. It is like one version of me is still there, still in her lap looking at her beautiful eyes. That car never stopped and I never left the car. The car went on forever and I lay in her lap forever.

I stay there, in her lap for an eternity, immortalised in time, with her looking out of the window and me being able to see her chin, her beautiful golden brown and silver hair. That me still smells the familiar stench of hospital mixed with the smell of her perfume.

I stay there frozen in time, waiting for the airport to arrive. It never will.

The Microcosm of the Belief System

Everything is theoretically impossible until it is done

Perhaps the only thing which gives me a bit of solace is in the fact that we are all going to die. It's surprising that everyone you've ever spoken to, thought of, will speak to, will all be dead by the turn of the century. We age and die. Perhaps what gives me solace is the fact that we are now due for a mass extinction event after the K-pg event[82] roughly 65 million years ago. Perhaps what gives me solace now is that Maa died before she could feel the anthropocene[83] extinction or the Holocene[84] extinction.

---

[82] the K-pg event - The Cretaceous Paleogene extinction event around 66 million years ago in which most of plant and animal species disappeared from Earth. This is the most recent mass extinction event on earth.

[83] Anthropocene – the current geological age where human beings are the main driving force and protagonists.

[84] Holocene – The present age and the interglacial age after the last epic Ice age (not the movie, but the original one)

Or perhaps, we are living through it right now! Why not? Perhaps what gives me solace is the fact that, out of the trillions of stars we have out there, more than the amount of sand grains we have on planet Earth, we are just a speck of dust and in that speck of dust, we humans, convinced that we are the asked predators, occupy only a very tiny or puny position. It gives me peace that we are small, literally on a cosmic scale and it gives me peace to think that the cosmos doesn't care if a little transaction of elements gave birth to the first life on earth, or a little transaction of elements gave birth to Maa or a little unfortunate transaction of events killed the woman I loved the most or a little transaction of events, made it possible for me to give you this message. The cosmos just doesn't care. We are not big enough for it to care about us and we never will be, even when after the Holocene extermination, there would be no humans, probably, and the earth would be standing all alone bearing the brunt of the solar storms, due to the depleted solar storms then increasing our core temperature to hundreds of degrees making it equal to Venus, turning it from a once beautiful home to a raging inferno. Scary? Right? No! Absolutely not! There's beauty in the way things unfold in the cosmos and I shall have it no other way!

Everything is theoretically impossible until it is done. Like say, no one knew humans would be able to fly. No one knew we would have cure for bacteria in the form of penicillin. No one knew, humans would actually go through this massive technological revolution, being able to merge space through a simple concept like video conferencing. No one knew drones would deliver medicines to remote villages in 2022. No one thought that Elon would develop a neural chip for the brain, much less own Twitter today. I knew living without Maa was impossible up until the 22 of March 2022. So yes, everything is theoretically impossible until we try or go through them.

Humans, of all subspecies, didn't realise that once their colonies would increase in size, they would need a better way to communicate than primitive signifiers and signifieds. Humans eventually developed language over thousands of years, at the same time, in multiple parts of the world. Humans have learnt to relate and associate with concepts and principles over thousands of years. Today I can convey all my stories to all of you, even to people I don't know, easily, through this colonial language, English, because (thank you Saussure for helping me with this part) you use the same signifiers in order to refer to the same signifieds. You know English, in short.

When Maa died, I cried more because I was afraid of the emptiness that would follow. I was afraid that I would die as a personality and would eventually have no emotions left. I was afraid that my grief would probably end up messing up all my other relationships, even Tulika. I was afraid because I was unaware of the future and unsure of what was to follow. We humans, are afraid of the unfamiliar and are simply put, complacent.

Fortunately or unfortunately, I wasn't in a black hole. I was not in another dimension where I was beyond the time space continuum. I wasn't able to walk into time like I walk into my bedroom or walk to the terrace. I was not able to encounter the future. I didnt know that life would go on. I did not know that Tulika, who was equally grieved that day, would suddenly need my support and would in turn support me a lot. I didn't know that Baba would emote (something I've never seen) and would need me. I didn't know that Baba would look at me, through lenses of Maa. I didn't know that the world wouldn't end, like it did in Don't look up[85]. I didn't know that today I would still be at Gurgaon, writing this, as time passes me by. And as time progresses, I'll discover a lot more about what I thought I wouldn't ever do, but still can!

There's before Christ and Anno Domini in the Gregorian calendar. We follow it faithfully because it allows us easier reference. I don't know why, but, I've been referring to many parts of my life as before maa and after maa. I look at things Maa had bought when she was alive and I keep terming them before maa things. I suddenly come across something I have recently purchased and I categorise them as after Maa. It's how I've been keeping myself busy. I've mentioned before how I was holding on to the last bits of chocolates Maa didn't eat, keeping them back for me and Tua. I ate them all. I decided to eat them, rather than microbes feasting on them and letting Maa's efforts of keeping them for me, go to waste. This was before Maa, as you can see! After Maa is a scary era. I'll

---

[85] Don't Look Up – a 2021 movie by Adam McKay depicting the story of apocalypse. Scientists predict an apocalypse but politics, red tapism and human instinct to disbelief leads them right to the extinction level event; the Holocene extinction.

have to relearn to do a lot of things on my own. Next time I got to a jungle safari, I'll miss Maa guiding me through flora and fauna. Next time I'm at the hills, I'll miss Maa reciting a poetry and then showing me picturesque landscape. Next time I'm at the sea, I'll miss Maa dancing with the waves. Next time I'm home, I'll inevitable break down because I'll never see her again. When I get married, Maa won't be there. Life has its own ways of bringing me fresh pain. I've been scavenging on memories of Maa, keeping them alive by reliving them. This is the after Maa era. Life will go on inevitably.

The Me That Never Was

Sometimes I wish I could talk to her

Death at childbirth was very common in the 1990s when the medical backbone in India was not at its best. Maa died when I took birth. I've only seen Maa in pictures but she seemed to be a happy woman. Even if I've been used to pictures of her, I've always imagined how she used to speak, how she used to walk, how she would hug me, feed me and talk to me, call me hers! The concept of Maa never existed for me, as Baba was everything for me, from the very beginning. I was premature at birth. I was definitely the reason Maa died, but my family wasn't illiterate. They knew what caused her death. They were prepared for it. I've always been treated as the miracle birth. They placed their faith on me; Baba, Amma, Kaku, Tua, Kakima and our extended family. They depend on me. It's been thirty one years and I've not known maternal care. I'm fine with it; I've been cared and loved a lot more than I imagine motherly love to be.

From the time I could speak and comprehend speech, I've been asked one question one too many times, "You don't have a mom?" to which I've always been apathetic and responded with a polite, "Yeah, no Mom". People have responded in multiple ways to that. Some have been extremely touchy about the situation like I don't have a leg or something. I kept feeling lost at why they would behave in such a way. I kept not understanding their reason for such behaviour. Some were too inquisitive and kept asking me how she died. I either answer them with the truth if I feel like they are not too nosy or just tell them...

"I wasn't there Uncle. I wouldn't know how she died"

"Beta, no one ever told you?"

"No uncle, never felt the need to know. I think it's better that way"

Yet some others empathised with my situation and gifted me smiles. And some others just did subtle "tch tch tch" (a subtle expression of contempt and regret in the Indian culture) and left the scene unnoticed.

Baba and Maa had a lot of picture together. I kept on looking at their images. They have so many happy memories of them up until when Maa was pregnant with me and she seemed like an angel; an angel who left after completing her task. I sincerely don't even know how she even sounded like. Thanks to being born in an underdeveloped country, Baba has no recordings of how Maa sounded like. There are no video recordings as well. Nothing! Nada!

I've seen how every other child is attached to their mothers. While they played with their mothers, I kept playing with mud and no one stopped me. While they kept walking holding hands of their mothers and fathers, on either end, I held my Baba's hand and saw the world, the

Catharsis with Maa

first time, up until now. While every other child brought their parents to their school, I either got Amma or Baba or even Kaku. Things weren't complicated at all. Unfortunately, people kept trying to empathise with me, I don't know why. They kept treating me as if I didn't have something in my life I needed a lot. I don't know what!

I've never been very touchy about not having Maa. It's what I was born with or rather, without. I had accepted it. I had structurally never had Maa. You never know what you lost, if you never had it in the first place. I've imagined how proud Maa would be at my results, or scolded me when I would score badly. I have imagined how Maa would treat my wounds when I would have fallen down in my maiden cycle ride. I've imagined how Maa would shout at me, to call me to her, for something and how she would hug me when she would see me after a long time. I have always imagined how Maa's voice would sound like and how her facial expressions would change when I would talk to her and make her happy. I've also imagined how Maa would look at me when I would get married. She won't be there but I've always imagined it anyway. I've never had Maa but I've always imagined how life would be like with her.

I've only heard how Maa was from Baba, from Amma and form others. Maa came to our family when she was very young, when Baba and Maa fell in love. She had always been the heart of the family, until she wasn't. Maa's smile was supposedly addictive. When she would speak, she would entice others into a deceptive yet beneficiary courses of actions. She was a wife, a friend, a philosopher and an amazing person! Statistically (from empirical surveys and spontaneous interviews with every person I've met in life) it seems like life would be better had Maa been around.

Sometimes I wish I could talk to her. Sometimes I wish I could have had an opportunity to know her. They say, she died a few hours after I took birth, from exhaustion, excessive bleeding and cardiac arrest in the end. I wish I had more time with her. I wish I had more time to have had hugs and kisses from her. I wish I had more time to have lived out my life in her presence.

As days pass by, I just rewrite my memories; only without her. I wish I had more time with Maa!

That One Time

A time which will never be or was

I woke up around 5.30 am this morning to her call. She ended up calling me because she was so content cheerful and gleeful that she couldn't hold it in.

"Tatai, I know you're sleeping. I won't take long."

"No worries Maa. Good morning. Why are you up so early?"

"I always wake up this early Tatai. You forget. So here's the deal. You remember the grapevine we planted last year? I can see grapes on it now. When you come back in summer you can have some sour grapes"

"What? They finally blossomed. That's brilliant. What did you feed it? Did you put some human shit into it or what Maa?"

"You disgusting fool. I gave it a used tea leaves, NPK, a lot of love and cared for it and it blossomed."

"Practically I have a feeling you can almost grow a redwood if you tried, in Chinsurah."

"You remember the Mexican vines and the trumpet vines too?"

"Yeah of course. The trumpet vines were the orange ones to the right side of our house, towards the water tank and the Mexican vines never grew."

"Not anymore. This morning, now, I'm right in the midst of orange trumpet vines and fiery yellowish orange Mexican vines. Not one, not two, but hundreds of them and the house is drenched in colours. I don't know what happened today, this week. The Bougainvillea have blossomed as well. But the biggest surprise Tatai is something else."

"You grew a dog out of a tree, didn't you?"

"Chup thaak (shut up, you imbecile). The seed balls that would never grow or do anything at all? Remember?"

"Yeah for the Jacarandas right? The ones you planted in the sand?"

"Yep, those. There's life. Eight out of twelve seeds have grown into saplings now. I can't believe it. It's taken months but now, finally they've grown into saplings. I now know how to grow them and I'll plant them in random places at Chinsurah. Ten years down the line, Chinsurah will have another colour, lilac violet in the midst of red, yellow, orange and greens."

"Maa that will take time. Why don't I help you out when I return? We can go out early morning and we can keep take your planter and plant it in safe places?"

"Yeah I would like that", Maa said with extreme relief as if this is what she was waiting for, for such a long time.

As the day progressed Maa called me multiple times to share even more plants that suddenly blossomed that day. The future is in constant flux and the past cannot be revisited (beyond the already existing langue we have created with the personal paroles of everyday life). The past if recreated, can sometimes change the future, which is the present we are living in now and that would make it the future past. This creates infinite possibilities or what we know as stringed universes which are created over possibilities, decisions and emotions.

She's somewhere watering her plants, getting excited over every bird that would come and sit at her terrace and at every new bud, every new flower she would see blossom.

She's somewhere reciting Tagore while she keeps looking at the setting sun. She's somewhere, keeping on with her infinitely scrolling Facebook feed, at times liking a few posts.

She's somewhere with me, travelling in my car, with Baba, Tua and Tulika. She's somewhere getting extremely pissed with patients who don't listen to her.

She's somewhere saying lives of patients and of plants. She's somewhere, still inspiring millions. She's somewhere hugging me, kissing my forehead.

She's somewhere sitting with our daughter, cooing with her, looking at her trying to figure out how much she looks like Tulika and how much like me, finally deciding that she looks like herself and not us. She's somewhere baking a cake for all of us.

She's somewhere, looking up at the sky, wondering at the magnificence of the Northern lights, as I stand by her holding her and holding Tua and Tulika, while Baba tries desperately to capture that. She's somewhere riding her scooty to a her work.

She's somewhere in all of us. Dear Maa, while you've successfully left us all, it's not the end. I love you Maa and someday in some crooked epistemologically ontological reality, I'll see you again.

Of Life and Death

Society thinks

Why did they have to burn her body? Why couldn't we just keep her body. A few days after her death, her body would be swollen and decomposed. The shine of her beautiful brown eyes, would be long gone and maggots would be feasting on her once beautiful soft flesh, I used to call my shelter. A few more days and all her flesh would have been fed on by bacteria, beetles, other scavengers, probably birds and other insects. What would be left, would be a skeleton; a skeleton devoid of religion, ethnicity, colour, race and creed. We have hurried our way into the work of nature and have created a systematic chain of command, we use, in order to dispose of once alive, now dead, bodies! We do not let them decompose. Loved ones, as society thinks, will not be able to bear the sight of their newly dead ones, slowly going through the process of natural decomposition; the process of slow decay and returning to star stuff. Society thinks that it's best to either let their flesh and bones burn away in an eternal carnage, we call a furnace or let them decompose underground, 6 feet away from the view of commoners. Society thinks, we are mostly weak, measly beings capable only of euphemising most things. But why do they have to burn the body though? I might have kept a piece of her bone, made a necklace out of it for me. Is it too much to ask? Is it too much that I'm asking to be made a bone out of my dead mother's bones; bones which have come out of a slow and long process of natural decomposition? Is this creepy? Does this scare you? Does this make you want to embrace religion? Does this warrant for you to use coercion such that no one does something like this? Does this hamper natural law?

I wish for them to have not burnt her body. I could've grown used to looking at her rotting body, slowly catering to nature in its own way. I could have cried all day and yet found peace in the fact that she returned to the elements. But in that one moment, everything was over. In that one moment, I knew it would be so quick that. In that one moment, all my senses were burning from over exposure to stimulus; I was overwhelmed. Looking at that pedestal slowly move into the furnace, with the person I loved the most made me sick from the inside. I wanted to puke. I wanted to jump over her. I wanted to stop her, to jump over her then dead body and not let go, but that that is not how societies work. That's not how things are supposed to be. I was pulled back. I had to let her go forever. I had to see her once warm body, slowly enter a carnage of eternal memories. I had to see her off, for the last time, never to see her again. I had to bid her the final goodbye. It was over.

How easy it would be, for me to just point Rick's interdimensional gun towards the other end and then jump over to another universe, just to find that Maa was just there, happily looking into my eyes. How easy would it be to abandon that universe, probably just kidnap myself and push me to the present universe and make my place comfortably in a universe where she exists. Why not? It is theoretically possible in any of the multiple stringed universes we are connected to and by. It is just an engineering problem now! Maybe someday. Just maybe someday, I'll see you again. Maybe someday I'll have that damned interdimensional gun I want so bad.

I'm a mere human. I cry every now and then. I cry every time I go back to her memories and I cry every time I remember her. I cry every day and yet no amount of crying will bring her back, not until I get that damned gun, not until someone makes a warmhole into parallel universes, and not until I become really well versed in impersonating myself in another universe with different nature and nurture. I just hope the laws of physics remain mostly same there!

That day I did not cry. That day I woke up surprised. I just remember rushing back home from Gurgaon. I just remember everything happening as they happened in the real world, before she died. I remember rushing my way into the hospital where she was being held and I remember seeing dad in tears. I held him while the doctors desperately tried to bring her back. A few moments later, a doctor came out looking sweaty and tired. Maa survived.

We all broke down into mixed emotions. We were happy and yet broken. We were broken knowing how helpless we, humans are. Fast forward to when she was taken back home and I remember her lying on my lap. I cannot but forget that smell of her skin like I remembered before. She was there, right on my lap, her hair flowing into my face. I asked her," Maa koshto hocche na toh kono? Kichu lokaccho na toh? Please bolbe Maa" (Are you feeling any pain? Are you hiding anything at all? Please talk to us whenever you feel anything is wrong Maa). I kept on looking into my phone as she slept peacefully in my lap. Baba sat on a chair, looking at us fidgeting with our phones and kept mumbling something to himself. It was all so real. I could smell the formalin-ish smell from her cloths, exactly like she used to smell. I could hear her talk, slowly and surefootedly like she used to. I could feel her touch, touch her myself. It was so real. It was so real, that I could not cry anymore. I just woke up and I looked around me, suddenly remembering it has been six months since she has died. It was so real...

The Eulogy No One Wants

Disintegrated into a million parts

We have all been eyewitnesses to deaths. Deaths are seemingly unwanted, undesired and yet they bring about an end, either sudden or gradual and meaningful to the narratives of people.

I have been privy to multiple deaths myself and while they have been mostly unpleasant experiences. Some found me partially leaving the death venues happy, while some deaths before Maa's were absolutely not needed. They either forced me to imagine myself in the positions of the ones who died or in the place of the dead.

It all started with the death of my Maa's Baba, way back when I was young. Then Dadu (Baba's Baba) died when Baba just got his job. Paritosh Mesho[86] died leaving Masimoni (Maa's elder sister) alone. Boro Mama died thereafter, followed closely by Dimma (Maa's Maa). The death toll keeps on increasing steadily till in 2020 when Bhulu Pisho (close relative of ours; his son was there to receive me at the airport on Day Zero) passed away and

---

[86] Paritosh Mesho – Masimoni's husband, who passed away.

then just like "Bayishey Shrabon" (22nd day of Sraban month, in Bangla calendar was the day Rabindranath Tagore had passed away) came 22 March 2022, when Maa left us all.

Maa will never see the Northern Lights. She died, never knowing how the Northern Lights actually look in person. If I ever have a child with Tulika, she will never know what our child will look like or how our child would refer to her.

Maa died not knowing that I would have asked her to dance with me, on my wedding day. Maa died without getting an opportunity to recite a beautiful verse from Tagore, at my wedding. Maa will not be in the pictures of my wedding.

Maa's body has now disintegrated into a million parts, all parts moving away from each other, like quarks did, after the big bang, from each other. Maa died not knowing that Elon[87] has taken over Twitter because he wants freedom of opinions and Maa died not knowing that one day, probably in the near future, she might have had the opportunity to sit inside a Tesla too. Maa died not knowing that the world cried for her, when she died. While she left our home for the last time, a big part of me, which loved her, died with her. It almost felt like that part of me, burnt along with her, when she died.

---

[87] Elon Musk – you really don't know Elon Musk? Tesla? Paypal? Space-X? Twitter? Ring a bell?

I have laughed again and I have smiled at times again, after Maa but every time I do, somehow I feel uneasy. I feel as if the happiness I feel then would be suddenly cut short by a swift bullet to the head by grief. I have also cried and broken down multiple times, when I have thought of her but I cannot wallow in my grief and crumble into pieces. I will laugh again. I will make memories again, without Maa, but I will keep her in my memories. Maa will live on through our memories. True, that she will never laugh with me again, never share my happiness again, never eat food with me again, never wake me up again and never love me again, never hug me again but my love for her will remain.

The last chapter, after this might be a figment of my imagination but also lets me end this novel on a happy note. This is how I would like to remember her. This is her legacy. The eulogy should have appeared at the end, logically but I have been told that I am not logical, many a times. Let me rightly remind you that I belong to a place (at least mentally and coherently) where time is not linked to space ,and time is just another dimension we may navigate.

Goodbye
Maa.

Once Upon a Time

The light at the end of the tunnel

I woke up in the morning. Baba called me around 8.30 am in the morning when I was already in the cab. Maa and Baba both spoke to me. They told me about their plan to go to Sandakfu a couple of days later, on the 12 of March. It's a beautiful place, at the foothills of greater Himalayas at a very high altitude. Maa wanted to be there for a long time. She wanted to see the majestic and humongous Kanchenjunga mountain from up close. Maa expressed her desire to be there.

"Your baba can click some amazing pictures of the mountains and we can also see some endemic birds there."

"Maa, is it really needed to go now? You said you'll come visit me in March or April. You take a leave now and you won't be able to make it to my place in the next two months. Don't do that. Come on Maa. Why don't we plan a trip to Sattal instead? Also, don't forget we planned on a trip to Norway after we get married, the next trip after my honeymoon with Tulika. You remember you wanted to see the Northern lights with me Maa? We can all go Maa"

"Tatai. Let me check. I really want to go to Sandakfu though. Sattal is a place I can always go to. Take me to other places near it too and I would love to see some birds. Last time your dad ridiculed me for collecting so many plants from there. Take me to the nurseries too, please"

"I will Maa. Will you come here then? Should I get tickets for you, Baba and Tua?"

"No no, not yet. Let me talk to your Kaku."

"I would love for all of you to come here. I can do my bachelor's trip with all of you"

All along, baba was smiling at both of us, deep into this conversation. The call was disconnected then. I smiled at the phone and went ahead with office that day.

Next morning, Maa called me.

"We are coming to your place. Will you be able to manage enough leaves Tatai? If you can't, it's fine too Tatai. We will take the weekend at Sattal? Will that be fine?"

"Maa I'll always take leaves for you. Moreover you earn three times my salary. I'm sure you can cover for the leave without pays I incur."

"Chagol" (stupid goat)

"So, should I purchase your tickets?"

"No Babui. I am already on it", said Baba from the side. The tickets were done and they were coming to visit me on the weekend with 14, 15, 16, 17 April, a long weekend with four holidays. I was happy, very happy.

Time starts to flow slowly, the moment you expect your loved ones to come, visit you. In the time till the day they came, I kept talking to Maa about all the plans I made for them and we were all excited. Maa kept telling me names of birds which she wanted to see there and the names of places where those birds would be. I kept noting them down and booked the rooms.

The day came soon. Maa, Baba and Tua had just landed in Delhi. It was the 10th of April, 2022. They sat in my car and we came back home. It was such a perfect Sunday. Everyone was happy and Tua kept being the joker she is, my loving joker! That night I slept beside Maa, with her hair falling on my hand. I grabbed her hand and she grabbed my hand back. Her warm fingers made me feel so complete. I could feel her breath on my hands. I looked at her sleeping and felt peace. I looked at Baba and I massaged his forehead. Then finally when everyone was asleep, I looked at everyone and found inner peace. This was what I wanted all along. I felt bad and guilty that I made Maa come to visit me instead of Sandakfu but in the end, she came to see me and I was extremely happy.

I remember the whole trip. It was so amazing. We even trekked to a place where we saw Paradise fly catchers. They were so beautiful and I remember Maa almost in tears, tears of joy when she saw them. We were also lucky that we saw the golden eagle up close. We saw a couple of owlets chubbing up each other, just like I, Maa, Baba and Tua slept together. We stayed in a wooden hut and it had a wooden fireplace. At night Maa kept singing and singing till we all got bored. We had chicken soup with roti at night, and while we were returning to our wooden room, this happened.

"Maa look up"

"What? Why?"

"Just look up. Tua, Baba, look up"

They looked up and they almost froze for a moment. We all eyewitnessed a moment of amazement. There was this subtle glow in the sky. The sky looked bluish green from lights in the horizon, lights from the side of Bheemtal. There was this subtle glow in the sky from that. Moreover, after the whole day at night, then, when the air density was highest due to cooling of temperatures, the clouds had finally reached a density higher than that of the air there and dropped down below the angle of vision, opening the night sky, first time for us to watch the balls of hydrogen burning for millions of years. We could see the clear night sky at that point in time and we were all amazed.

"Babui, can you capture this image?"

"Yes Baba I can try but it will never be as amazing as we feel it is right now. The picture of video we capture of this will never encode the emotion we are manifesting right now. The feeling of being like a little child looking at something for the first time, the feeling of having ice cream for the first time, the feeling of being in love for the first time, the feeling of looking at the earth from an aeroplane for the first time are all feelings we can never encode in a picture."

"Tatai, look, these are Northern lights for us. I guess Norway came to Sattal"

"Maa you're crazy. You've imagination beyond human. But for once, yes, the sky looks beautiful. They aren't the Northern lights but let's call this one our Desi Northern lights experience. "

The particles of dust in the atmosphere, there, had created a gradient of lights starting from dark blue to dark green, by acting like a super massive prism and by scattering the lights. Unlike the Northern lights, this was not a result of electronic disturbance in the air, or the result of liquid lightning as some claim but due to a rainbow like prism effect from far away lights, at night. In a matter of twenty minutes, I guess, the particles drifted away and the sky was dark again.

I will always remember this trip. This was one of our most memorable trips. Maa, me, Baba and Tua had the best trip of our lives. We laughed, we cried in joy, we fought over chicken pieces, we sang together and we stayed together. I shot so many drone videos of all of us that in the end I told Maa, I was bored with the drone.

I also remember our last conversation at the airport before dropping them off.

"Tatai, take care. I need you to be okay. You know right, that we care? And that we are always worried about you?"

"Maa, I will miss you all." I hugged them all together, with tears in my eyes. Maa tried hard to not cry but she couldn't.

Catharsis with Maa

She held me tight and kept hugging me.

"Babui, eat your food on time. Don't worry about money. We are there"

"Dada, I will see you soon", said Tua and I held her tight too.

I looked at Maa and then held her face, kissed her forehead. She kissed my cheeks gently, kissed my forehead too.

"Tatai, you be fine. Take care of yourself. Eat food you like, sing when you're happy, go out for a walk and watch the birds and flowers. Don't fall into a mechanical world and lose your individuality. I love you Tatai. We will see you soon Tatai. Don't cry. As long as we are there, you don't have anything to worry about. You're getting married soon and soon you'll have new responsibilities. You've grown up to be a man I always wanted to raise you as. You've made us proud and you'll keep doing so. You always keep on telling me that I earn a lot more than you. Money isn't everything. Respect is. I take pride in telling others, you have that. You've acquired that. I love you Tatai."

"When do I see you again", I asked them all.

"Tatai, pagol chele (you crazy boy). We just met you. I will see you soon Tatai".

And then Baba, Tua and Maa, slowly faded into the airport doors. They looked back at me one last time through the glass doors and I smiled at them, with tears in my eyes. I gestured them goodbye. They slowly vanished into the airport and tears came down my warm cheeks, cooling them.

"Goodbye Maa", I muttered to myself.

I imagined Maa slowly fading into the horizon, slowly fading like a piece of beautiful music slowly blending into the environmental noise. I felt her fade into the Northern lights like sunlight fading into the horizon after six months of daylight due to the 23 degree Earth's tilt. I felt Maa disappear like dry petals of flowers crumbling in a strong wind. I felt Maa leave like when E.T. left in the film. I felt like she had left, finally, and yet I didn't know she was gone. I felt like she was gone and yet she was right there still hugging me. I felt like she would always remain in my body since I was a part of her body. I was her legacy. I am, rather, not was. With a heavy heart, I started driving back home. Maa was tired after the day. She was sleepy. She will sleep as the flight takes off I thought. The road was empty, dark, dimly lit and even though I was always bad at goodbyes, I went back home, sad yet happy, with a heavy heart yet content; as if having found some sort of deep closure to a long standing regret; as if finding peace after millennia of pain. In the end, I found relief.

" I love you Maa. Goodbye", I whispered to myself...

And This is to Go Beyond

I don't mean for you to read or watch more but you may find these interesting

I have put in suitable annotations in the form of footnotes but the following might add to the understanding of the book better.

Tyson, N. D. (2019). *Letters from an Astrophysicist*. Random House.

Hawking, S. W., & Hartle, J. B. (1972). Energy and angular momentum flow into a black hole. *Communications in mathematical physics*, *27*(4), 283-290.

Fuentes-Schuller, I., & Mann, R. B. (2005). Alice falls into a black hole: entanglement in noninertial frames. *Physical review letters*, *95*(12), 120404.

Saathoff, G., Karpuk, S., Eisenbarth, U., Huber, G., Krohn, S., Horta, R. M., ... & Gwinner, G. (2003). Improved test of time dilation in special relativity. *Physical review letters*, *91*(19), 190403.

Dettmer, Philip. (2021). Immune a Journey into the Mysterious System that Keeps You Alive

Cosmos: A Spacetime Odyssey by Carl Sagan

Cosmos: A Spacetime Odyssey hosted by Neil deGrasse Tyson

StarTalk by Neil deGrasse Tyson

www.ingramcontent.com/pod-product-compliance
Lightning Source LLC
LaVergne TN
LVHW061609070526
838199LV00078B/7219